THE KABBALAH

A STUDY OF THE

TEN LUMINOUS EMANATIONS

FROM

RABBI ISAAC LURIA מהאר״י ז״ל

THE KABBALAH

A STUDY OF THE

TEN LUMINOUS EMANATIONS

FROM

RABBI ISAAC LURIA מהאר"י ז"ל

WITH THE COMMENTARIES SUFFICIENT FOR THE BEGINNER CALLED

SECTION I	SECTION II
INNER LIGHT	INNER REFLECTION
Direct commentary: explains word by word all subjects contained herein by the "Ari ז"ל" with superb clarity and simplicity, in a divine image which transcends time, place, material ideas and objects, and in a style lucid enough for the beginner.	General commentary: deals with a wider, general explanation of all subjects contained herein, making the Literature of Kabbalah accessible to the student in an easy, figurative language that enables a transmission of spiritual concepts.

An explanatory glossary of questions and answers is provided.

by RABBI YEHUDA L. ASHLAG ז"ל

Compiled and Edited by

DR. PHILIP S. BERG

VOLUME II

CIRCLES AND STRAIGHTNESS

RESEARCH CENTRE OF KABBALAH
JERUSALEM – NEW YORK

The publication of this volume
has been made possible through
the efforts of

MR. EDDIE SITT
New York, N.Y.

TABLE OF CONTENTS

Preface   i

SECTION I

PART 1

Chapter 1   The Line as a narrow pipe   3

        2   The extension of Light into the void   7

        3   The Circle is not attached to the Endless   9

        4   The Endless surrounds at a distance   12

        5   The Emergence of the Ten Circular Sefirot   14

        6   The Line connects all the Circles   26

        7   The Secondary and Tertiary Sefirot   31

        8   Closer and Farther of the Circles to the Endless   34

PART 2

        1   Emergence of the Ten Sefirot of Straightness   38

        2   Five divisions of soul of Lower Man   41

        3   Surrounding and Inner Light, Outer and Inner Vessel   43

        4   The Light of Circles and Straightness   47

        5   Long face illumines Father and Mother of Circles   50

        6   Primordial Man   56

        7   Vessels of Straightness follow Circles   58

SECTION II

Chapter 1 The Ten Sefirot of Circles   62

2 Primordial and Aby''A   68

3 Essence and Material of the Vessels   76

4 Four Aspects of Impurity   81

5 Restriction and the Curtain   91

6 The Curtain and the Returning Light   98

7 Purification and Emergence of the Five Levels 102

8 Drawing and Clothing of the Vessels   109

9 Primary, Secondary and Tertiary Sefirot   115

10 Binding by Striking   130

Table of vocabulary questions   134

Table of topical questions   137

Table of answers to vocabulary questions   143

Table of answers to topical questions   161

Other RCK Publications   186

PREFACE

Since the writing of my preface to volume I some three years ago, it is with mixed feelings that I now attempt to add to that which has already been said.

In reviewing the spiritual developments of the past three years, one hardly takes notice of the *implications* or goals of campus unrest, the drug scene, or for that matter world harmony or rather the lack of it. To understand that which takes place upon the stage of metaphysical (spiritual) *history* in the upper realm, one need merely observe the scene enacted on our mundane, physical level. Have we come any closer to solving the one basic problem around which all other problems revolve; namely, the humanities complex? Is man capable of living with his fellow man, or are we still consumed within the *effectual* syndrome of basic root problem; i.e., poverty, discrimination, housing, ecology...

Almost forgotten are the *effects* of unrest and world dissention, and man has gone back to his slumbering abode, attempting to solve his daily *existential* problems that immediately surround him. Whereas, the effectual problems appear clearer, more dramatic than the cause; the root problem remain seemingly unclear because of our veiled position. Merely displacing problems does not solve anything. It just creates a vacuum which is subsequently replenished with other danger signs. And so the daily struggle goes on, never taking into account the fact that as long as the "root" problem is not removed, the "branches" of problems will still flourish.

[i]

The colors, faces, and places may change, but never the basic problem. Although the branches may fade away, the root still remains firm, one generation to another. The cause of the problem has not been solved.

The left-wing of yesteryear is considered the right-wing of today, all succumbing to the advancement or modernization of the "times". And so it has been since time immemorial; the condition of right and left constantly emerges as a divisive factor, never change but for the faces, places, and dates. Then from what and to where does this trip of advancement lead, if at the end of the road a similar scene appears? The cry of "we need a change" or "society is not sensitive to the needs of the people" almost appears as a broken record. Violence of today simply reflects the mood and external picture of the times. It comes and goes. Yet, we all fall prey to these slogans, with the next slogan appearing to solve man's ills where the previous one failed.

Is it possible that man may find it so difficult to solve the one common problem of the entire world, or of a nation, city, and even a household—the problem of human relations; while at the same time, technologically speaking, it appears that man has all the potentiality of solving such intricate problems in any scientific endeavor? Can one question the strides made in all fields of science, whether it be medicine, space, electronics, or telecommunications.

How many times have we heard the knowledgeable scientist assert the following: "Present the problem and I will solve it?" And true to form the solution is found. While this does not preclude the fact that the solutions have only been the forerunners of subsequent problems. Or that technological advancements which solve todays problems will be outmoted by the progress of tomorrow-missiles, anti-missiles, anti-anti-missiles... But my question is the following: Why can't the scientist find within the present those solutions of the future? Why must he be caught up in the never ending race of time, space, and motion which necessarily incurs the trial and error process which so unrealistically involves such heavy expenditures of man-power, financial resources, and nerve-wracking decisions only to be shortly effaced with the on-coming of that invitable long bearded man called "time". Might we not be wiser were we to stop progress for a moment and reflect briefly on what might actually be the root problem of any endeavor, rather than tackle each and every seemingly time consuming problem, merely for the sake of removing one problem to replace it by a score of others? Sometimes it almost appears as one walking up a down escalator. With each step forward the individual finds himself in the same position if not one step behind! Before undertaking a project will the scientist realize and ask of himself; "What is the *final* goal and what is the solution to the *final* problem?"

Man appears to be the master of all these intricate challenges, yet a seemingly trivial matter of his desire to live in a world of ease, without frustration, disappointment, or even unfounded fears appears beyond his grasp. Wherein lies the problem? I stress the "problem" rather than the accepted and commonly used venacular, "wherein lies the answer" because the root of our inability to solve the basic and most pressing problem lies not within the realm of sufficient answers to our problem; but rather in our inability to understand the "basics" or root of the problem.

For those of you who have come to understand the first volume of *The Ten Luminous Emanations*, the verified existence of metaphysical veils has been established. Furthermore, the conclusion of most psychiatrists that the mind of an individual operates at more or less of 50% of capacity or ability, inevitably must be a source of our inability to understand a problem from beginning to end. This, subsequently, must prevent us from realizing a final solution which would encompass all of the ramifications from beginning to end.

With the foregoing in mind, it is of no wonder that we as individuals, or the world at large, find ourselves in a disarray of social, economic, and ecological standards which almost defy the human mind. How does one grasp or learn to detect the root problem from the numerous incidental problems that constantly seem to creep up? How does one cut through the maze of never ending veils which prevents a thorough insight to the very end?

To understand this thoroughly we must remove some of the basic misunderstandings that surround our mode of logic.

We have learned that the first three Sefirot are known as "Crown", "Wisdom" and "Intelligence".

Now let us explain why they are called by these names: the Root is called Crown because it is not clothed in the Vessels of the Emanation but rather encircles and surrounds its Vessels from the outside, and "Crown" is, etymologically, "something that surrounds." The first phase is called Wisdom because from it are drawn the Wisdom of the Torah, and all other forms of wisdom found in the world, in their final phase. And our sages (may their memory be blessed), have already explained this term very well, saying: "Who is wise? He who

sees what is born.'' (Masechta Tamid, page 32). This means:
as soon as he looks at something he perceives what will be
born and proceed from it, i.e., he sees all the future consequences of the thing observed, to the very last one. For
example: when one says that a doctor is a great wise man,
what this really means is that at whatever disease he looks
he is able to see all of the possible results to which it may
lead, to the very last one. Similarly, when he looks at any
medicine he grasps completely all of the results this particular
medicine might have on the body of this patient, and so on.
In the same way the natural scientist, when he looks at some
natural substance, sees all of the possible ways that substance
could combine with the rest of nature, and all the possible
results of these combinations. Thus in all branches of wisdom:
every definition of wiseman or complete wisdom is simply a
form of: ''seing what is born,'' from each and every detail
of existence, right to the last result.

From this, one also may learn the true definition of ''Intelligence,'' for the entire ''power of Understanding'' refers
to the ability to ''see what is born'' from every detail of
existence—whether in the Holy Torah or secular domain—all
this is drawn from the Sefira of ''Intelligance'' and therefore
is called Intelligence. From the Sefira of Kingdom comes the
phase of control by absolute power and compulsion, analogous to the fear of the (secular) kingdom, and therefore called
''Kingdom.'' The remaining Sefirot will be explained below,
in their appropriate places.

One may not, however, question the preceding explanation
in the following way: If so, then the Sefira of Intelligence had
to exist before the Sefira of Wisdom, for a longing and medi-

tation on seeing what is born precedes and causes the final completeness which is seeing what is born, called Wisdom. But I have already explained that the order of the Emanation of the Worlds is the opposite of what would seem logical, the fulfillment of the Desire preceding and causing the revelation of the Desire (see above, Q, begin.: "The Desire to Receive"). The fulfillment precedes and causes the revelation of Unfulfillment, for in this manner the degrees are evolved and descend from the Endless, PB"G, in Contraction or Restriction after Restriction, until this world, the most spoiled of all.

In other words, the term "problem" actually denotes the "unfulfillment" which is the dominant cause or motivation of the "desire" to fill the particular need called "unfulfillment." Let us take for example, one who decided to enter the medical, scientific, or legal professions. What was the *root cause* or motivation for this decision? Parental, economic, environmental influences or simply desire for the profession which developed within the individual have been given as possible causes or reasons for the selection of a particular vocation. Now, to satisfy a root cause, one must, from a Kabbalistic viewpoint, examine the cause so as to ascertain that this motivating factor proves satisfactory in each and every single instance, irrespective of time, space, and motion. Parental: there has been some cases, if not in most instances, where the parent did not attempt toin fluence a child as to which profession is best suited for him. Thus, it is quite apparent from a logical standpoint, that the reason (parental) is not a *root* reason and subsequently, relying on this premise would merely be an exercise in futility. This mode of reasoning only places us within the mistaken belief that *symptomatic* reasoning vis-à-vis prevailing condition is the determining factor to be reckoned with. But it is the very reasoning that is constantly subject to change, and consequently, any solution geared to the prevailing condition must lose its effectiveness as the cause changes or even disappears. Thus the reason of parental influence, economics, or environment are not to be considered *root* causes for no other reason except they do not apply in all cases. It is for this reason that Kabbalah gears its study to the understanding of the *root* cause which is not governed by change of time, space, or motion. This will be the sole cause for all cases in a given situation.

If we are now reconciled within our mental framework that the existing approach to finding solutions is a fruitless operation, we are now on the threshhold of a new dimension in determining the root of a problem and its final solution. The information provided by the study of Kabbalah can and will bring about the absolute solution.

The Zohar contains all of the root characteristics of each and every single physical manifestation existing in this mundane world. Whether it be in the field of medicine where the total clarity of each part of the human body is defined— (e.g. bone structure, muscle fiber, or organ placement) or in any other scientific field including space, telecommunications, computer, metallurgy, psychiatry... The Zohar elaborates not merely on the "discovery of" composites or "how" they operate; *but equally, if not more important,* on the "why" of their functions. Knowing all to well the manpower, time, and expenditure spent on research and development into the unknown of the foregoing, one could well imagine how best served mankind might be were *their efforts* directed to the elimination of costly ventures. The Kabbalah furnishes this vitally needed information to aid mankind in his quest for a more in-depth understanding and ensure the desired solutions to all of man's ills or "unfulfilled desires." Not with make-shift trial and error methods, which may or may not be effective, but through the knowledge of Kabbalah new vistas are provided to this approach to comprehension of the known and unknown. By eliminating the efforts and expenditures of research into the known elements of this universe, man may have the opportunity to embark upon the road to understanding the metaphysical where the "action" really takes place.

To revert back to man's 50% ability of mind, the Kabbalah states that no physical system of communication, as highly developed as it might become, will ever equal the effectiveness or efficiency of man's built in telecommunication system. In fact, the ultimate goal in the study of Kabbalah is to educate and train the individual in this personalized communication system so as to enable ourselves to "tune in" with each other without the atmospheric disturbances that inevitably exist in all physical communications systems. The Five Books of Moses are the physical manifestations of our mundane world similarly to the physical systems of our society. What gives far more clarity to the Bible is solely the Kabbalah which uses the Bible as a basis for its beginning in this endeavor to reach the plane of metaphysical communications.

This form of communication has already been well documented by experiments conducted at Duke University in the United States. While informed individuals no longer doubt that information may be transmitted by nonphysical methods, the understanding of the "how" and "why" remains a mystery. Here again, the study of Kabbalah clearly demonstrates its ability to logically explain the unknown of "how" and "why". E.S.P. (extra-sensory perception), the awareness of the mental state of another individual, telepathy, and other forms of metaphysical communications or transmissions is *crystallized* beyond any form of contradiction within the Zohar. Without the benefit of this information, we almost compare this lack of knowledge to the understanding of the cable system of electricity without comprehending the "current" itself due to the lack of ability of the five senses to perceive it. While all systems are "go", the non-detected element of motivation remains unknown. The Zohar is to the Bible what the current is to the wires; i.e., the soul to the body.

Is there any doubt of the result that might be achieved if there were true and pure transmissions of messages between man and his fellow man avoiding atmospheric disturbances?

We are well aware of the simple fact that when one speaks on the telephone the voice transmitted no longer sounds the same as the individual transmitting. This is the effect of physical substance on non-physical entities. Herein lies the root of man's problems in the humanities—we need a pure, unadulterated true system of communication. Compounded is the problem when mind and heart are distorted in transmission of thoughts.

Another form of communications is missiles and anti- missiles systems. While space prohibits the elaboration of the root of these systems, nevertheless, the entire subject is described in detail in the Zohar, in the sections related to the holiday of Rosh-Hashana, which is one of the concepts contained in Rosh-Hashanah. The blowing of the Shofar is by far the most potent force available as an anti-missile in destroying and diffusing "warheads."

When after tremendous expenditures of money and manpower, our space scientists speaks of "gates to heaven" and all of its ramifications, again, this subject is clearly defined in the Zohar, thus leaving very little room for exploration and experiments. Why is it when the astronaut leaves the earth's atmosphere, he is no longer influenced by the earth's power of gravity? We know the existence of and accept this phenomenon; but the "whys" are yet unexplained.

From the foregoing it might appear that we are heading towards a non-physical reality and our entire cosmic universe is "one great production of thought rather than a great machine, or so is the hope of Kabbalah to give man these clear insights.

Many of us are familiar with the Biblical story of the Patriarch Jacob and his twelve sons. One rarely questions the importance or possible lack of significance of "why" were there twelve sons and not eleven or thirteen. In addition, *why* was Joseph singled out as the son to whom so great a portion of the Bible is devoted? Is this, in fact a mere story; or are there deeper implications to every word or even every letter of the Bible? The Zohar emphatically states: "were these simply stories with no deeper meanings, then I am certain we might find many individuals who can weave far more interesting tales than appear in the Bible." Subsequently, the Kabbalah, reveals the deeper insights to the implication of Joseph and all other stories in the Bible.

The twelve sons of Jacob refer to what is known as the

Zodiac. This is the significance of the number twelve. Furthermore, why Jacob and not Isaac or Abraham, or for that matter "why" any part of the story is the way it is, is thoroughly explained in the Zohar. The Zohar also informs us that our Patriarch Abraham, was the first known Astrologer any many of the tales revolving around Abraham concern themselves to a great extent with the subject of Astrology.

When a Kabbalist discusses the days of Creation these are the questions we are apt to ask: "If the Lord is as all powerful and all inclusive as established religion would lead us to believe, why then was it necessary for the Lord to need six days in which to complete His work?" Wouldn't one day or for that matter one second be sufficient? Secondly, this seventh day of rest doesn't appear to be acceptable. If we are referring to the Creator, then was He so exhausted after six days of "work" that He needed to rest on the seventh day? Here again, the Zohar reveals the inner meaning of Creation and clearly proves that physical interpretation of these actions are unfounded. It explains that the word "day" refers to a given sephira which indicates a particular line of communication in its' development through the process of cause and effect. The seventh day is indicative of the type of atmospheric conditions, which relate both physically and metaphysically to the effect of total completion of Creation, or the end development of the sixth Sefirot.

Without some insight into reincarnation our psychologists, psychiatrists and astrologers will rarely even after extensive expenditure of time and energy, reach the root problems. Kabbalistically, we know that a symptomatic cause such as environment *never* determines the characteristics of an individual. While it may prevent a person from perfecting his inner problem or "unfulfillment" nevertheless, this is not "root" cause. Remove the environmental factor alone, and a solution will not be found. For example, a child with a tendency to steal, placed among thieves will undoubtedly find it difficult to correct this impairment. Placing this same child in an environment of integrity, without the benefit of rehabilation will not reap the desired effect. The same holds true for our drug problem. The mere removal of drugs, as a solution or their availability of them, is not a *root cause* of this problem. For drugs have always been available. The root cause or this unfulfillment of a need for spiritual satisfaction is the true cause.

On the lighter side of the coin, we are now experiencing a movement known to most of us as "Women's Liberation". One merely has to refer to the Kabbalah in relation to reincarnation and you will see clearly the "why now" answers to this and all other "modern" movements.

The tremendous interest found in many circles of people in relation to various forms of meditation is described, as well as what truly is meditation. Kabbalistically, we take this to mean "tuning in" with a transmitting station in the hope of receiving from a higher spiritual station. The famed Kabbalist, Rabbi Isaac Luria, the "Lion of Safed," found it necessary to author two voluminous works on meditation alone, using the Zohar as his source material. Why is there a necessity for having such an extensive thesis on this subject? But to paraphrase, an oft-repeated expression of the Kabbalah; if one seeks to attain metaphysical knowledge, he merely has to observe the physical manifestations which surround his daily activities. One knows all to well that a desire to hear a particular radio program, if the transmitting station is not operating at that given time, there will be no broadcast. Therefore, one can only "tune in" when those wave lengths are sending. While we have at times the desire to receive via our own "receiving sets" the Light of Spirituality sorely needed at a specific time, must always be governed by the transmitting stations schedules and whether it is operating or not. Similarly, as our space exploration has indicated that the "gates of heaven" (the invisible gates that either permit or prevent objects to pass through) are not penetrable at all times, so is meditation regulated by metaphysical forces beyond our control. Therefore what we do need is a time-table of when we can "tune-in". This is but a segment of the knowledge included in Rabbi Isaac Luria's work on meditation.

Secondly, extensive research into the need for superior materials to act as cables for transmission has yielded some materials as unacceptable and others as acceptable to meeting the task. During meditation, one should be well equipped with proper metaphysical conduits to ensure a "loud and clear" reception. If the cable is not sufficient treated, reception might be weak or none at all.

Thirdly, bearing in mind that a high quality "receiving set," produces superior reception, so it behooves an individual seeking spirituality through meditation, to improve his "receiving set." Again, this is adequately elaborated upon by Rabbi Isaac Luria, and inevitably will lead to partial or total removal of our dormant 50%.

The absolute physical laws of nature that govern, as we understand them, work similarly within the confines of the non-physical. It is in this particular area where we find the study of Kabbalah significantly different from other metaphysical studies. Laws governing within the realms of the metaphysical must not and cannot oppose those mechanical laws of our universe. Consequently, while our scientists devote their time and energy in the exploration of the physical universe, it might seem a far better choice to expend this very effort in understanding the root causes of our universe which reside within the phase of the metaphysical.

With regard to the field of medicine, we hear a great deal of reference made to the psychosomatic causes of disease. In fact it has more or less been agreed upon that about 90% of all ailments may be attributed to psychological causes. If this be the facts, than it is incumbent upon the medical profession to exert their efforts into this area. Psychosomatic causes and related cures to such ailments are totally defined and described in the Kabbalah; with the advantage of "root" causes rather than symptomatic effects. Where inadequate answers to the "whys" in medicine have previously prevented many breakthroughs the Zohar concerns itself primarily with the root function of the body. Subsequently, there is less need of observing the symptoms, when one can almost forecast the path of an ailment prior to the oncoming of the symptoms. In other words, the mere observance of metaphysical changes that are present in an individual give immediate insight to the oncoming of disease, prior to the actual symptoms. Let us take for example a new born infant. The pediatrician or obstetrician, when first observing the infant, will stretch his hands across the new-born's chest separating the infants arms. The reflex action in a normal infant is the immediate drawing together of both arms, whereas the lack of this instinctive reflex indicates a malfunction in its neurological makeup. This is what is commonly called a moral reflex. Furthermore, if a hand of a new born is pried open a normal grasp reflex will occur. Again, if this is not the case, a neurological malfunction is indicated. While this has become a normal procedure for all newborns by pediatricians, nevertheless, the "why" or root cause has never been thoroughly ascertained. Kabbalistic interpretation is that without a normal metaphysical root called "desire to receive", which is indicated by its physical manifestations called branches; the manifestation in the branch will always be in harmony with its principle root source. Consequently, one aware of the root is already provided with the yet unknown future manifestations. Without an understanding of the root source, the "why" will remain obscure.

We are presently witnessing a great deal of interest in the Far Eastern philosophies and cults, indicating an upsurge in the search for spiritual development and attainment. A great deal of energy has been spent to determine the origin of the Far Eastern philosophies. The Zohar anticipating this question answers it as follows: Genesis, Chapter 25:6 "But unto the sons of the concubines which Abraham had, Abraham gave gifts; and he sent them away from Isaac his son, while he yet lived, eastward, unto the east country." The Zohar questions the meaning of the word gifts, and replies as follows: "The word 'gifts' refers to the stages of spirituality which do not include the 'emendations' and subsequently these people (sons of the concubines) moved eastward to what is known as the Far East. Hence the word eastward to the בני קדם

people of the Far East.''

Another subject described in detail in the Zohar is metals and inanimate objects. While seemingly inconsequential motivations within inanimate properties may appear to the five senses, scientists, nevertheless, are well aware (through experimentation provided by trial and error apparatus) that various chemicals or metals behave differently under varying circumstances. But, when one peers through the Kabbalah, the ''root'' function of each and every single inanimate object is lucidly described. Subsequently, how these properties will behave under future conditions may well be perceived if the function at root source is known in advance. According to the Zohar, the root function of gold is negative, meaning that its property consists of the receiving quality which dominates over its positive or imparting quality. Subsequently, an alloy with gold would necessarily have to consist of an opposite characteristic. Again, all the seemingly difficult qualities of metals are totally explained in the Kabbalah, as it is an all inclusive study.

At the present time, so many of us have become attached to our scientific mode of life style since within the realm of science heretofore phenomena have become realism. This attachment to the thought form which one develops, however good and even scientific, has nevertheless placed many of the metaphysical principles of the root system which have withstood the test of time, space and motion, in the background. This is in addition to the recognized liabilities that have occurred as a result of scientific developments. Needless to mention is the lack of the humanities within the confines of scientific research. For the scientist engages himself on the level of the physical which unfortunately eliminate the basic tenets of the metaphysical because of the obscurity and mystery surrounding its concepts.

The awareness of Kabbalah as a single potent force in man's striving for better human relations has never before been recognized by so many. This has been a great source of strength to all of us at the Research Centre of Kabbalah and it has given us the courage and stamina to continue pressing forward until the goal of "peace on earth and good will towards men" has been fully realized. Of this we are certain, someday in the near future, our men of science will acclaim the Zohar as such a knowledgeable source of truth and information which in turn, will contribute towards this very goal.

For this reason Volume II of the *Ten Luminous Emanations*, is appearing prior to our volumes on "the introduction to the study of Kabbalah and Zohar." Volume II contains a great fountain of material for the scientist in the hope that some open minded people will apply the knowledge contained in this voume to establish the validity of the material presented. If this volume aids in making Kabbalah, acceptable root source scientific information, then we at the Centre firmly believe that our task will have taken a giant step forward. The volumes on "introduction" will ultimately finalize our dream of bringing the "truths" of Kabbalah to all. It is this that will bring about the final solution to mans' complex problems of the humanities, and he will once again find himself living in harmony with his fellow man.

DR. PHILIP S. BERG

SECTION I

PART 1

Explaining the Ten Circular Sefirot that were revealed after the Restriction, surrounded by the Light of the Endless, and how these Circular Sefirot receive Light from the Line. (containing eleven topical divisions):

Chapter 1
The Line is like a narrow pipe.

Chapter 2
a) The extension of the Light of the Endless into the void;
b) The extension was gradual.

Chapter 3
The Circle is not actually attached to the Endless; it is connected to it by means of the Line.

Chapter 4
The Light of the Endless surrounds and influences the Circle at a distance.

Chapter 5
a) The Line is called Primordial Man;
b) The order of emergence of the Ten Circular Sefirot.

Chapter 6
The Line connects all of the Circles.

Chapter 7

a) Every World and every Sefira is composed of ten secondary and tertiary sefirot, etc., *ad infinitum*;

b) The Circular Sefirot surround one another like the skins of an onion.

Chapter 8

The closer a circle is to the Endless, the higher and loftier it is. And so this world, which is farther from the Endless than all others (because it is situated at the Middle Point), is the most lowly and corporeal of all the Worlds.

CHAPTER 1

THE LINE AS A NARROW PIPE

The Line (A) is like a (C) single narrow pipe (B) in which the waters of the Upper Light of the Endless World (D) extend and are drawn to the Worlds in the air and the void.

* (א) (א) וקו זה, כעין (ב) צנור דק (ג) אחד, אשר בו מתפשט ונמשך מימי אור העליון (ד) של אין סוף, אל העולמות, אשר במקום האויר והחלל ההוא.

INNER LIGHT

A) This is the Line that was extended from the Light of the Endless, Praised Be God, into the void after the Restriction (see above, volume 1, chapter 2, B).

B) The Vessels of the Ten Sefirot of Straightness are called "Pipe" or "Pipes" because they limit and control with great precision the paths of the Light drawn through them, preventing the Light from spreading out in any way other than that designated by the shape of the Vessels; as, for instance, the pipe which limits quite precisely the waters which pass through it, so that the waters pass through in the shape of

* עץ חיים, היכל א' ש"א ענף ב'.

the pipe, whether narrow or wide, without any change whatsoever in their shape. For the same reason the Lights which pass through these pipes are called the Ten Sefirot of Straightness, for they are drawn according to the laws of these pipes, straightwise and true; that is to say, the more important **Light** is clothed in the purer vessel, and so on, without any variation whatsoever, because of the powerful confining control that the pipes exercise over them.

The power of control exercised by these pipes exists because every thing that is Desire on an Upper Level is Necessity on a Lower Level emanated by its Upper Cause. Therefore, that Restriction on the fourth phase found in the Circular Vessels with respect to free will becomes, in the case of the Vessels of Straightness created by them (Circular Vessels), a phase of power and control which constrains them. This power is called "Mesech" or Curtain, as explained below.

This is the mystical meaning referred to in Tikun Zohar of what we read regarding Restrictions: "Reverse רצון (desire) *RZN* and you will find צנור (vessel) *ZNR*." As we have said: the "Pipe" acting as a Curtain (which implies a Restriction of control, i.e., checking its Desire to receive in the fourth phase from the Upper Power which controls it) is really the opposite of the material of the vessel itself whose essence is "the Desire to Receive," for it prevents itself from fulfilling its own Desire. Thus you will find in all the commentary which follows that whenever we wish to refer to or stress the disappearance of the Light from the fourth phase we refer to the Restriction. When we wish to stress the power of the additional Restriction with regard to the Light of the Line which did not extend to the fourth phase we refer to the "Curtain," which is the power that prevents the Light from spreading to the fourth phase. When we are speaking about the Vessel in general, i.e. the Vessel and Curtain together, we use the term "Pipe." And when we speak about the Light, the Vessel, and the Curtain together, i.e., the Light clothed by the measure of the pipe, we use the term "Line." When we speak of a Vessel without a Curtain we use the term "Circle."

C) Our Rabbi's (Ari) precise use of the word "single" is meant to exclude the Emendation of the three Lines in the World of Emanation. It teaches us that in the world of Primordial Man there is still no Restoration of three Lines, but only of this "Single Line". The reason for this is that the Restoration of the three Lines was accomplished afterwards, in the world of Emanation, and was drawn from the cooperation of the attributes of Compassion and Judgment (as was explained in the appropriate place), and here we are dealing with the world of Primordial Man, and the aforementioned cooperation has not yet occurred; thus we have here only a single Line.

The entrance of the Light to the Receiving Vessel of the Emanation is termed Extension or Spreading (see the *Table of Answers*, volume 1, 14), and it has already been explained above that the Receiving Vessel in the Emanation is termed Pipe. (N.B. above).

D) There is a recognized order distinguishing the stages of the birth of the Partzuf, wherein the four phases of Desire to Receive are termed: Light, Water, Firmament, and One

Hundred Blessings, or One Hundred Gates. This is because of the reversal of the Lights. For because of this change the Light receives the image of water, as is explained elsewhere. Our Rabbi (Ari) teaches us that the root of this matter involves the entrance of the Line, for the emerging Light (in the form of the Line) is distinguished (as against the Upper Light) in the form of "Water." And this is why it says precisely: "The waters of the Upper Light of the Light of the Endless," for with the extension of the Light into the narrow Pipe the Light is diminished in its value in the Endless and takes the form of Water.

CHAPTER 2

THE EXTENSION OF LIGHT
INTO THE VOID

When the Light of the Endless was drawn in the form of a (E) straight line in the void referred to above it was not drawn and extended (F) immediately downwards, indeed it extended slowly—that is to say, at first the Line of Light began to extend and (G) at the very start of its extension in the secret of the Line it was drawn and shaped into a (H) wheel, perfectly circular all around.

ב) והנה בהיות אור הא״ס נמשך, בבחינת (ה) קו ישר תוך החלל הנ״ל, לא נמשך ונתפשט (ו) תיכף עד למטה, אמנם היה מתפשט לאט לאט, רצוני לומר, כי בתחילה הת־ חיל קו האור להתפשט, ושם תיכף (ז) בתחילת התפשטותו בסוד קו, נתפשט ונמשך ונעשה, כעין (ח) גלגל אחד עגול מסביב.

INNER LIGHT

E) Light which emerges according to the laws of the four phases, step by step, that is to say, from pure to the thick or impure and then stops at the fourth phase is called "Straight Line."

F) Do not err by interpreting the "immediately" and "slowly" used here to refer to chronological order, for the

Spiritual is above time, as is known, but instead, "Immediately downward" means without a change of degrees, and "slowly" means by evolution of degrees. This refers to the linking of the order of the four phases discussed, as is explained below, later on.

G) Meaning the "Root" of the extension which is revealed and called Line. Since it is a new emanation it has a distinct Root (called the Sefira of the Crown of the Line) which illuminates it in its revelation. And from this Crown the Light of the Endless extends to the Line, in the four phases mentioned: phase 1 called Wisdom, phase 2 called Intelligence, phase 3 called Beauty, and phase 4 called Kingdom. And about this order Our Rabbi (Ari) says "it extended slowly;" for at first the Crown emerged, next Wisdom, next Intelligence, and next Beauty, and so on. (see the *Table of Answers*, volume 1, 8, the interpretation of the word "next.")

H) For the meaning of the word "Circle" see the *Table of Answers*, volume 1, 41. See also volume 1, chapter 1, 100. And when the Light of the Line is dressed in the Circle it is called "Wheel."

CHAPTER 3

THE CIRCLE IS NOT ATTACHED
TO THE ENDLESS

This Circle was not (I) attached to the Light of the Endless encircling it on every side. (J) If it were, it would return to its former extent and be nullified in the Light of the Endless, and its power would cease to be manifest, all becoming Light of the Endless, as at the outset. Therefore, this Circle is near the Circle of the Endless but is not attached to it. The (K) essential binding and juncture of this emanated Circle with the Emanating Endless is (L) by means of the Light of the Line mentioned above which descends from the Endless to influence it.

ג) והעגול הזה, היה (ט) בלתי דבוק עם אור הא״ס הסובב עליו מכל צדדיו, (י) שאם יתדבק בו, יחזזור הדבר לכמות שהיה, ויהיה מתבטל באור א״ס, ולא יתראה כחו כלל, ויהיה הכל אור א״ס לבד כבראשונה. לכן העגול הזה סמוך אל עגול א״ס, ובלתי מתדבק בו. (כ) וכל עיקר התקשרות ודבי־קות העגול הנאצל ההוא עם א״ס המאציל, (ל) הוא על ידי הקו ההוא הנ״ל, אשר דרך בו, יורד ונמשך אור מן אין סוף ומשפיע בעגול ההוא.

INNER LIGHT

I) That is to say: all of the Light in the Circles is received only through the Line, which illumines as a new phase of illumination, having only three phases, as said above—in this way it differs from the Light of the Endless which encircles it in the form of Circular Light (see volume 1, chapter 2, C). This is why Our Rabbi (Ari) writes: "not attached" to the Light of the Endless, which is to say that the form of the Circular Light of the Crown of Circles is not equivalent to the Light in the Endless for similitude of form is attachment (uniting) in the case of Spiritual Substances (see the *Table of Answers*, volume 1, 12, and see also *The Inner Light*, volume 1, chapter 2, A, beginning: "From this..."). That which "Encircles" means that which causes.

J) That is to say: if its illumination were also in all four phases as is the case with the Light of the Endless, then its image would be equivalent and attached to the Endless, and it would be nullified in the Endless indistinguishably.

K) The Light which emerges from the Endless to the Emanation is called Straight Light, and this Light is bound up with the Emanation by the clothing of Returning Light which goes out from the Curtain and upwards with the power of Coupling or Binding by Striking, (as will be explained more fully) called "Binding," for this Returning Light which ascends from the Curtain of the fourth phase from the Straight Line grasps and takes hold of the Upper Light into a Circle. This works in such a way that in a place where the Returning Light does not clothe the Upper Light this Upper Light is considered, with respect to the Emanation, as if it did not exist, for it cannot grasp it without this clothing called the Returning Light. This will be explained further below. It is like, *mutatis mutandis*, a tallow candle: even though its main strength of illumination derives from the tallow in the candle, nevertheless the Light could not be bound to the tallow without the wick, and when the wick is consumed then the candle is extinguished, even though much tallow might remain.

L) The reason for this is that there is no Curtain in the Circles to enable the Returning Light to ascend, and without it there would be no binding of the Emanation with the Upper Light, as said above (see E, above). There we are told that the Vessel of the Line is termed "Pipe," far more inferior than the Circular Vessels which were revealed with the first Restriction, before the arrival of the Line (see below for explanation). Therefore Our Rabbi (Ari) teaches us that although the Circular Vessels are much superior than the Line, nevertheless they receive no Light whatsoever on their own, instead, for the reason cited, they must receive all the Light they contain by means of this Line which is so much more inferior than they.

CHAPTER 4

THE ENDLESS SURROUNDS
AT A DISTANCE

And (M) the Endless encircles and surrounds it on all sides, for it too is circular, (N) but at a distance (as explained above). For it is imperative that the illumination by the Endless of the emanations be only by means of the Line, otherwise, if the Light were extended to these emanations through their surroundings, they (O) would be subsumed by the Emanator, without (P) defining borders.

ד) (מ) והא"ס סובב ומקיף עליו מכל צדדיו, כי גם הוא בבחינת עגול (נ) סביב עליו, ורחוק ממנו, כנ"ל. כי הוא מוכרח שהארת א"ס בנאצלים תהיה דרך קו ההוא לבד, כי אם היה האור נמשך להם דרך גם כל סביבותיהם, (ס) היו הנאצלים, בבחינת המאציל עצמו, בלתי (ע) גבול וקצבה.

INNER LIGHT

M) In each Sefira we distinguish two types of light: Inner Light and Surrounding Light, for the Light clothed within the Sefira is called Inner Light, and the Light which is unable to be clothed within the Sefira, remaining distinct in its Root because of the existing boundary, and receiving its illumination at a distance, is called "Surrounding Light." And Our

Rabbi (Ari) teaches us that although the Circles are distant from the Endless, that is to say, there is a great change in form between them, nevertheless they receive a phase of illumination from it at a distance, called the Surrounding Light, which illuminates in two ways: general and particular; and so סובב "encircles" refers to the Surrounding Light (general) and מקיף "surrounds" refers to the Surrounding Light (particular).

N) This teaches us that this Surrounding Light that the Circles receive from the Endless illuminates and encircles them from all sides. That is to say from all four phases, even the fourth, where the Inner Light does not shine. Nevertheless it receives illumination at a distance by means of the Surrounding Light from the Endless. The reason for this is explained by the fact that with respect to the Endless: "... it too is in the form of a circle," in other words the Light of the Endless is called Circular Light because it does not distinguish between phases, illuminating and filling the fourth phase as well (as stated above, volume 1, chapter 2, C). Therefore its illumination reaches the fourth phase of the Circles as well but from a distance, as explained.

O) See above, J.

P) The Restriction and the Curtain on the fourth phase which prevents it from receiving Light is what establishes a "Boundary" for the Light, for it limits the extent of its extension so that it stops at the boundary of the fourth phase. The total received by the Emanation, diminished by the Restriction, is termed "Limit."

CHAPTER 5

THE EMERGENCE OF THE
TEN CIRCULAR SEFIROT

This (Q) first circle, the one more closely bound up with the Endless, is called the Crown of Primordial Man. Afterwards, the Line was further extended and (R) drawn a bit more and then turned back so that a (S) second circle was formed within the first circle. This is called (T) the Circle of Wisdom of Primordial Man. The Line continued to extend further downward and turned on itself once again to make a third circle within the second circle. This is called (U) the Circle of Intelligence of Primordial Man. In this manner the Line of Light continued to extend and turn back upon itself until the tenth circle, the Circle of the Kingdom (V) of Primordial Man, was formed. Thus is explained the concept of (A¹) the Ten Luminous Emanations or sefirot which emanated in the mysterious

ה) והנה (פ) העגול הזה הראשון היותר דבוק עם הא״ס, הוא הנקרא כתר דאדם קדמון, ואח״כ נתפשט עוד הקו הזה (צ) ונמשך מעט וחזר להתעגל (ק) ונעשה עגול ב׳ תוך עגול הא׳, וזה נקרא (ר) עגול החכמה דאדם קדמון. עוד מתפשט יותר למטה, וחזר להתעגל, ונעשה עגול ג׳ תוך העגול הב׳, ונקרא (ש) עגול בינה דאדם קדמון. ועל דרך זה היה הולך ומתפשט ומת-עגל, עד עגול יוד, הנקרא עגול מלכות (ת) דאדם קדמון. הרי נת-באר ענין (א) היוד ספירות, שנאצלו בסוד יוד עגולים (ב) זה תוך זה.

form of (B^1) ten concentric
circles.

INNER LIGHT

Q) It is necessary to understand the distinctions in the
names of the Ten Sefirot for at times we term them the four
phases, and at times we term them: Individual, Living, Soul,
Spirit, and Life, and at times we term them: Crown, Wisdom,
Intelligence, Beauty (which includes six sefirot in itself) and
Kingdom. The fact is: when we speak specifically of the Vessels that is to say with regard to the material of the Emanation
alone, we name the ten sefirot they contain in terms of the
four phases in the Desire or Will to Receive (see above). But
when we are speaking specifically about the Light which is
clothed in those vessels, in that case we term them: Life, Spirit,
Soul, Living, Individual. And when we speak of the Vessels
alone, but wish to emphasize the Residues or Impressions of
Lights which they contain when they are devoid of the Light
related to them, then we call them: Crown, Wisdom, Intelligence, Beauty, and Kingdom.

The source of the ten Vessels mentioned above, termed
Crown, Wisdom, etc., is in their immediate distinctions in the
World of the Restriction before the entrance of the Line, after
the withdrawal of the Light of the Endless from the ten sefirot
for these ten Circular Vessels remained devoid of Light as
stated above. It is clear that although the Light withdrew from
them, nevertheless there remained in each and every Circle a

form of Residue from the Light that was in it. That is to say: a very small illumination from the total of the former light remained in each vessel, and it is this remaining illumination that induces a longing in the Vessel that prevents it from resting or achieving stasis until it draws in all the Light it once had in quantity and quality. This illumination is called "Residue." One should know that the names for the Ten Sefirot: Crown, Wisdom, etc., define mainly the Residues of Lights which remained in the ten Vessels.

From this one may learn that no Desire can be imagined in the Worlds not even the slight stirring of Desire (whether in the Upper or Lower Worlds), even amongst the silent (rock), the growing (flower), the living (animal), or speaking created beings (man), unless it be rooted in these Ten Circular Sefirot. Furthermore, it is also to be understood that it is absolutely impossible that any Desire be stirred up in Existence unless at an earlier time a fulfillment was revealed sufficient to that Desire.

The Desire to Receive is not the first cause of the Light or its fulfillment (already well explained in the first volume), as men think; instead, the exact opposite is the case: the Light and the Fulfillment are the cause of the Desire for the Desire to influence necessarily included in the Upper Light gave birth characteristically to the Desire to Receive in the Emanation. For whatever is Desire in the Upper Worlds becomes Potential and Necessity in the Lower Worlds (N.B. above). Thus the Upper Light became a cause for the revelation of the four phases in the Desire of the Emanation, these being the roots of all the Desires revealed in the various Worlds. Therefore:

how could any Desire appear without a cause—that is, without this Upper Light which gives birth to it? It would be like saying that there is a creature in the world without a father and mother who brought it into being. It is already known that in the Endless are already extant and established all reality and all the creatures worthy to inhabit the worlds with all of their future growth, final beauty, and perfection destined to be revealed on their behalf in the worlds. (As thoroughly explained in *The Inner Reflection*, volume 1, 11). Moreover, already in the Endless, all of the Desires destined to be revealed have come out and were revealed, and were also completely and finally fulfilled. It was the completion and fulfillment—this being the attribute of the Upper Light—which gave birth to and revealed these Desires. Thus the fulfillment of the Desire precedes and causes the revelation of the very Desire related to this fulfillment—as explained.

Now one may well understand the matter of the Residues which remained in the Ten Circular Sefirot, after the Restriction and withdrawal of all the Completion and Fulfillment which were in these four phases called Ten Circles. The meaning of these Residues is that they were well "residenced" or impressed and engraved with all the Desires which they were full of when they were in the Endless but have now lost, and so they remain of necessity desiring and longing for all these Fulfillments and Completions that they once had. These are what we term: "Residues."

This is what was meant by what was said above: no revelation of Desire of any Essence (either in the Upper Worlds or in the material world) can be imagined that is not rooted in those Ten Circular Sefirot. There are two Roots prior to the existence of all the worlds after the Restriction: the one when every Desire is already found to be completed in all its beauty and fullness [this is the existence the Root led in the Endless, Praised Be God (PB''G)]; the other: when all the Desires stand completely empty of their previously related Fulfillments from the Endless—this is called the World of the Restriction, and all the vessels and material of creation are drawn from the World of Restriction; only empty vessels, to be sure, and Desires which have lost their Fulfillment, as stated above. All the Fulfillments of these Desires are drawn from the Endless, PB''G. Remember well these two facts, for they are of the utmost importance, and must be remembered for any further study of this Kabbalistic Wisdom.

R) Do not err by interpreting that it was "drawn" in space and dimension, Heaven forbid. Rather, everything which thickens and is impurified in this way is said to be drawn from above to below, for the Pure is distinguished by being above; and the impure, by being below. This is reckoned by the closeness of the form to the fourth phase, for everything closer to the fourth phase is distinguished as more impure, and everything far from it is distinguished as more pure. Thus, "and drawn slightly" means that it was impurified somewhat, and the word "drawn" refers to the Light of the Line.

What is meant by this drawing is that in each and every Sefira are found ten Sefirot, whether we examine a Sefira of the Ten Circular Sefirot, or a Sefira of Ten Straight Sephirot. When the Ten Sefirot of the Sefira of the Crown emerged, at first the Line emerged in the form of its first three Sefirot, called the Head of the Crown of Straightness, and its illumination extended to the Sefira of the Crown of Circles, which also is composed of Ten Sefirot, as stated above. These Ten Sefirot of the Crown of the Circles encircle (cause) only the three first sefirot of the Ten Sefirot of the Crown of the Line. Afterwards, that is after the Ten Sefirot of the Crown of the Circles have been absolutely completed, then "the line extends further," "and is drawn somewhat"—that is to say it sent out its seven lower Sefirot to complete the Crown in the Ten Sefirot of Straightness. In this way the seven lower Sefirot of the Crown of the Line were drawn downward, i.e. they impurified more than any of the ten Sefirot of the Crown of the Circles, and so these seven lower Sefirot are not encircled by any Circles, for all the Circles are above them, i.e. purer than they are. We have already said that "above them" means "purer than they are."

The reason for this you may understand from what was explained above (letter L): the Circular Sefirot precede and are much more important than the Sefirot of the Line, for the Circles have no form of Curtain whatsoever. This Curtain, found in the Sefirot of the Line, stands in the middle of the Sefira, at the last phase at the Head of the Sefira, in other words at the last phase of the first three Sefirot of the Ten Sefirot of Straightness which are found in each and every Sefira of Straightness (as stated above), also called the Head of that Sefira. When we said that the Curtain is included in the Sefirot of the Line this referred to the seven lower Sefirot of each Sefira which are found below the Curtain, and this is not the case with the first three Sefirot of the Sefira, those called Head, which have no share of Curtain since they are located above it. Therefore these first three resemble entirely the Ten Circular Sefirot, for both of them have no phase of Curtain, and therefore they are in one phase, and the Ten Sefirot of each Sefira of the Circles encircle the first three Sefirot of each Sefira of the Line. However, the seven lower Sefirot of each Sefira of the Line located already below the Curtain (the Curtain included with them) are much inferior to the phase of the circles, and since we know that anything inferior is lower, therefore they are distinguished by being found below all Ten Circular Sefirot, and no phase of Circles can be found in the place of these seven Sefirot, since the Circles are more important than they are, and far superior to them, as explained.

It has been thoroughly explained that there is empty space between each and every Circular Sefira; to the extent of seven Sefirot of the Sefira of Straightness found there, for all Ten Sefirot of Circles of the Sefira of Crown encircle only the first three Sefirot of the Crown of the Line, however the seven lower Sefirot of the Crown of the Line are drawn down below all Ten Sefirot of the Crown of Circles. After the seven Sefirot of this Crown of the Line are completed the first three Sefirot of Wisdom of the Line begin to emerge, around which circle all of the ten Sefirot of the Sefira of Wisdom of Circles. Thus, between the last phase of the Crown of Circles and the first phase of the Wisdom of Circles there is empty space in which are found the seven lower Sefirot from the Crown of the Line, which do not have circles encircling them; in like manner, between Wisdom and Intelligence (there is empty space etc.), and so on with all the Sefirot.

S) One must be especially careful here not to be confused by the figurative descriptions of dimension and place in discussing Straightness and Circles. They are adduced because of the necessities of language—remember in all that follows that Straight illumination means the light enters vessels which have a Curtain on the fourth phase, and encircling illumination means that the light enters vessels which do not have a Curtain on the fourth phase. Remember, however, that although the Vessels of Circles do not have a Curtain on the fourth phase, nevertheless the fourth phase is unable to receive any illumination therefrom after the first Restriction because all of the Light contained in the Circles must be received by illumination through the Line, which is Straight illumination. (As stated above, L), and the Light of the Line does not illuminate the fourth phase at all, being drawn by the power of the Curtain, as explained. Thus the lack of Light in the fourth phase of the Circles is not because of the Vessels, which do not have a Curtain, but rather because of the first Restriction which controls them, and since the first Restriction is not distinguished by lack (see the *Table of Answers*, volume 1, 83), therefore all four phases of the Vessels of Circles are equal in value, without any distinction between small and large (as explained above, volume 1, L). All of the darkness in phase four is thus on account of the Light received from the Line by which the fourth phase is not illuminated as explained.

Moreover, you may now understand that after the Circles received the Light by means of the Line there were established amongst them (by means of this receival) differences of degree, small and large, in the Ten Sefirot of the Circles as well. For Beauty is larger and more refined than the fourth phase which is Kingdom, for Kingdom has no Light and Beauty has Light, since it is the third phase, and the Sefira of Intelligence of Circles has more Light than Beauty, being further away from the fourth phase, since it is the second phase, and so on. However all of these degrees are not on account of Vessels but on account of the Light of the Line which is received— remember this.

T, U) It has already been explained that these are the names of the four phases: their Root, which is the Desire to influence included in the Upper Light is called Crown. The first extension to the Emanation, i.e. the first phase, is called Wisdom, the second phase is called Intelligence, and the third phase is called Beauty, or, the six Sefirot: Mercy, Judgement, Beauty, Lasting Endurance, Majesty, Foundation. The fourth phase is called Kingdom. It was also explained that only when we are speaking about the first substance in them, only then do we term them the four phases and their Root. However, if these four phases are already included with the phase of Residue as they were in the World of Restriction, then we term them: Crown, Wisdom, etc., as was so thoroughly explained above.

Now let us explain why they are called by these names: the Root is called Crown because it is not clothed in the Vessels of the Emanation but rather encircles and surrounds its Vessels from the outside, and "Crown" is, etymologically, "something that surrounds." The first phase is called Wisdom because from it are drawn the Wisdom of the Torah, and all other forms of wisdom found in the world, in their final phase. And our sages (may their memory be blessed), have already explained this term very well, saying: "Who is wise? He who sees what is born." (Masechta Tamid, page 32). This means: as soon as he looks at something he perceives what will be born and proceed from it, i.e., he sees all the future consequences of the thing observed, to the very last one. For example: when one says that a doctor is a great wise man, what this really means is that at whatever disease he looks he is able to see all of the possible results to which it may lead, to the very last one. Similarly, when he looks at any medicine he grasps completely all of the results this particular medicine might have on the body of this patient, and so on. In the same way the natural scientist, when he looks at some natural substance, sees all of the possible ways that substance could combine with the rest of nature, and all the possible results of these combinations. Thus in all branches of wisdom: every definition of wiseman or complete wisdom is simply a form of: "seing what is born," from each and every detail of existence, right to the last result.

From this, one also may learn the true definition of "Intelligence," for the entire "power of Understanding" refers to the ability to "see what is born" from every detail of existence—whether in the Holy Torah or secular domain— all this is drawn from the Sefira of "Intelligence" and therefore is called Intelligence. From the Sefira of Kingdom comes the phase of control by absolute power and compulsion, analogous to the fear of the (secular) kingdom, and therefore called "Kingdom." The remaining Sefirot will be explained below, in their appropriate places.

One may not, however, question the preceding explanation in the following way: If so, then the Sefira of Intelligence had to exist before the Sefira of Wisdom, for a longing and meditation on seeing what is born precedes and causes the final completeness which is seeing what is born, called Wisdom. But I have already explained that the order of the Emanation of the Worlds is the opposite of what would seem logical, the fulfillment of the Desire preceding and causing the revelation of the Desire (see above, Q, begin.: "The Desire to Receive"). The fulfillment precedes and causes the revelation of Unfulfillment, for in this manner the degrees are evolved and descend from the Endless, PB"G, in Contraction or Restriction after Restriction, until this world, the most spoiled of all.

V) The first world to be emanated after the Restriction is called the World of Primordial Man, also called the World of the Crown. The four worlds: Emanation, Creation, Formation, and Action clothe this Primordial Man.

A¹) And even though they are merely four degrees, i.e., the four well known phases, nevertheless they have Ten Sefirot, this on account of the third phase, called Small Face or Beauty, which contains 6 Sefirot: Mercy, Judgement, Beauty, Lasting Endurance, Majesty, and Foundation; the reason for this will be explained in the proper time.

Here one must understand the precise locution found in the *Book of Formation* (Chapter 1, 44): "Ten, not nine." This teaches us a very notable thing, since it has already been explained that all illumination of the Sefirot is from the Upper Light, even the Circles, which are equal, do not illuminate the fourth phase, called Kingdom. The name Sefira refers to Light and Vessel together, that is to say Upper Light clothed in a Vessel, but a Vessel without Light is not so named, for "Sefira" signifies brightness and luminosity; one might think that Kingdom is not a Sefira, Heaven forbid, since the Upper Light does not illuminate it, as explained. Therefore, the author of the *Book of Formation* says that there are precisely ten, and not nine Sefirot (Heaven forbid), for Kingdom is also considered a Sefira, the reason being that every binding of the Upper Light with the Ten Sefirot is by means of the Returning Light which Kingdom elevates from below to above by means of its Curtain (see K, above). Therefore, quite the reverse is true, it being the most exalted of the Ten Sefirot, for without it the Light would not be bound with the Upper nine Sefirot, as explained. For this reason it is thought of as if it were completely composed of Light. Understand this—it will be further explained in the proper place.

B[1]) See volume 1, *Inner Light*, chapter 1, S.

CHAPTER 6

THE LINE CONNECTS ALL THE CIRCLES

All of these circles are (C¹) connected by means of the narrow Line which extends from the Endless through (O¹), down (E¹) and drawn (F¹) one circle after another until they are all perfected (G¹) and completed. Through this Line flows the Abundant Light which each and every circle requires.

ו) והנה (ג) הבחינה המחברת כל העגולים יחד, היא ענין קו הדק הזה המתפשט מן האין סוף,(ד) ועובר (ה) ויורד (ו) ונמשך מעגול אל עגול, עד (ז) סיום תכלית כו־לם. ודרך הקו הזה, נמשך האור והשפע, הצריך לכל אחד ואחד מהם.

INNER LIGHT

C¹) This means: we already know that there is a gap of empty space between each of the Ten Circular Sefirot, as is characteristic of the seven Sefirot of the Illumination of Straightness in that Sefira (as explained above, R, begin: "It has been thoroughly explained..."), however there is no such gap between the Ten Sefirot of the Line which begin from the Light of the Endless and extend to the Middle Point, which is the fourth phase, called Kingdom, beneath which there is no further phase, as explained. Because the first Ten Sefirot extend from the Endless in the mystical form of a Straight Line (also called the Ten Sefirot of Primordial Man) there is no gap between them whatsoever. Therefore Our Rabbi (Ari) says that the Sefirot of the Line also link the Ten Circular Sefirot for this is the mystical nature of the Lower (Seven Sefirot) in each Sefira of Straightness: it binds the Ten Sefirot in the Upper Circular Sefirot with the Ten Sefirot in the Lower Circular Sefira. The illumination of the Ten Circular Sefirot of Wisdom by the first three Sefirot of the Straight Sefira of Wisdom of necessity, the light (the first three Sefirot) passes through the seven lower Sefirot of the Straight Sefira of Crown, for the first three Straight Sefirot of Wisdom must receive illumination from the seven Straight Sefirot of Crown and influence the Ten Circular Sefirot of Wisdom. And so the seven lower Straight Sefirot of Crown link the Ten Circular Sefirot of Crown with the Ten Circular Sefirot of Wisdom, and so from Wisdom to Intelligence, and so on, in like manner.

D¹) This means that the Line, a straight illumination, acts as if it breaks the roofs of the Circles and passes through them, and descends and is drawn to the end, which is the Middle Point. To be sure, however, this does not refer to space and dimension; one must know, in order to understand this, that there is no revelation of Light in the Worlds, whether above or below, without it being drawn from the Endless, PB"G, which is above the Restriction; the Light must devolve from and pass through all of those degrees and worlds found between the world in which the receiver of the revelation of light is found and between the Endless which is above the Restriction.

We already know that there is no disappearance of Spiritual Substance, and so it is absolutely impossible to say that this revelation of renewed Light which devolves through the various degrees disappears from the first level or degree when it comes to the second, and disappears from the second when it comes to the third, as is the case with something material which passes from place to place; this is not at all the case with something spiritual which is not subject to disappearance. Rather, of necessity, it remains at each and every level as it passes through and its coming to the next degree or level is analogous to the lighting of one candle by another, the first candle not losing anything at all. In such a way the revelation of Light which comes to any level in the World of Action, has already benefited all of the levels in the Worlds between the Endless above the Restriction and the receiver in the World of Action.

Therefore, the illumination of the Straight Line must pass through the Vessels of the Circles since the phase of Vessels of Circles preceded the Line, for the Vessels of the Circles came out at once with the Restriction, but the Vessels of Straightness came out afterwards with the Line, therefore this illumination which passes between them never really moves from its place, since as was stated, there is no disappearance of Spiritual Substance.

Furthermore, one must understand that in the matter of the devolvement of the Light from place to place there are two forms of remnant in the places traversed: the first is "permanent remnant," which means the mixing and binding with the Light already found at the level, the two Lights becoming

one, as if they had always been one; the second is merely
"temporary remnant," in other words there is no mixing and
binding with the Light found there, with both Lights then
becoming one, instead, the Lights stay distinct. Our Rabbi
(Ari) teaches us that the Light of the Line which traverses
the levels of Circles does not do so as "permanent remnant,"
but merely as "temporary remnant," to teach us that it is not
mixed with the Light of the Circles to form one phase, rather
it is found there distinct, and in its own phase. This is why
Our Rabbi (Ari) says so precisely: "And [it] passes"; understand this.

The reason for this is that the Light of the Line precedes
the Light of the Circles, for the Circles receive their Light only
by means of the Light of the Line, therefore the Light of the
Line is far more important than the Light of the Circles, and
therefore it is not mixed with the Light of the Circles, as said
above. The Light of the Line is called Light of the Spirit, and
the Light of the Circles is called Light of Life.

E¹) All extension of Upper Light to the Emanation is
termed descent, which means that as it extends it becomes
progressively impurer. We already know that the more pure
is termed "above" and the impurer is termed "below," and
so since the Light becomes progressively impurer in the course
of its extension, therefore it descends from above to below.

The reason for this impurifying which the Light undergoes
on account of its extension is because the extension follows
the order of the four phases: it begins at phase 1 and continues until it touches the Curtain found at phase 4. It im-
purifies progressively because the first phase is the purest, the

second phase next purest, and so on to the fourth phase, the impurest of all (see volume 1, chapter 1, N, begin.: "The reason").

F¹) The illumination of Straightness is expressed by: "And is drawn…" and the illumination of Circles by: "encircles," (above, R).

G¹) This is the fourth phase of Circles, called the Middle Point. This is the one termed the material globe in this world. The form of emanation in the world of Primordial Man was extension to this mundane world; but after the second Restriction (called the World of Points) the conclusion of Emanation of Primordial Man was elevated to the form of a point of the World to Come, whose place is distinguished as higher than the world of Creation, as will be explained in the proper place, with God's help.

CHAPTER 7

THE SECONDARY AND
TERTIARY SEFIROT

Each and every World has ten primary sefirot, and each and every sefira in each and every world (H[1]) has ten secondary sefirot of its own; all, like the (I[1]) layers of an onion, one inside the other, in the manner of the wheels pictured in the Sifre Tohniyim.

ז) והנה כל עולם ועולם יש בו יוד ספירות פרטיות, וכל ספירה וספירה פרטית שבכל עולם ועו־ לם, (ח) כלול מיוד ספירות פרטי פרטיות, וכולם (ט) כגלדי בצלים זה תוך זה, על דרך תמונת הגל־ גלים כנזכר בספרי תוכניים.

INNER LIGHT

H[1]) The reason for the inclusiveness of the Sefirot one may understand according to the well known principle: there is no disappearance of Spiritual Substance, and so all the Light which passes from place to place secures an eternal place in all the phases it traverses, as written above, D, begin.: ("This means that...".) Since each lower Sefira is emanated from a higher, in the manner of cause and effect, therefore each lower Sefira is considered as traversing the higher.

Therefore, of necessity, all of the Sefirot are included one in the other. For example: When the first two Sefirot emerge, Crown and Wisdom, indeed, the Light of Wisdom must emerge from the Endless, PB''G, since all is drawn from it and afterwards the Light of Wisdom must traverse the Sefira of the Crown before coming to the Sefira of Wisdom, since the Sefira of Crown caused its emergence. Since the Sefira of Wisdom has passed there, it secures a place there, and now we find two Sefirot in the Crown, i.e. Crown and Wisdom. In this manner, when all Ten Sefirot of the Upper Light emerged from above to below, until Kingdom, the nine Sefirot below Crown had to pass through Crown since it was the first cause of their emergence. Therefore all of them secured a place in it, since there is no disappearance of Spiritual Substance, as said above, and therefore all nine Lower Sefirot are in the Crown itself, because they have traversed it (as explained).

In this manner there are, of necessity, nine Sefirot in Wisdom, since the eight Sefirot below it had to pass through it, as explained with respect to Crown. Similarly there are eight Sefirot in Intelligence for the same reason, and seven Sefirot in Mercy, and so on, with one Sefira in Kingdom since it is the lowest of all the Sefirot.

We know that Kingdom sends upwards Ten Sefirot of Returning Light which clothe the Ten Sefirot of the Upper Light, called the Ten Sefirot of Straight Light. This Returning Light is called Light of the Kingdom, which has no other Light. This Returning Light is in all places termed Ten Sefirot ascending from below to above. See the *Inner Reflection*, volume 2, chapter 6, 66, where it is explained that the Kingdom is called the Crown of these Ten Sefirot because it is the cause of their emergence, and the Sefira near it is called Wisdom, and the third level is called Intelligence, and so on. We find that the purer is also the smaller, until the actual Crown receives from this Returning Light only the phase of Kingdom (N.B. below).

Therefore, we know, the Ten Sefirot from below to above are all found in the Kingdom, for all of them pass through the Kingdom, since the Kingdom is their mutual root; therefore each of them secured a place in the Kingdom and we thus find that the Kingdom as well consists of ten Sefirot. Through the Sefira of Foundation pass the nine Sefirot of the Returning Light. Indeed, Foundation contains ten Sefirot: one Sefira of the Upper Light, which is from above to below, and nine Sefirot of Returning Light, from below to above, which must traverse it. Similarly, with respect to the Ten Sefirot of Majesty: Two Sefirot from above to below, these being the Light of Majesty and the Light of Foundation which passes through it, and eight Sefirot from below to above. Similarly, with respect to the Ten Sefirot of Lasting Endurance: three from above to below and seven from below to above; and so on, in the same manner. After the emergence of the Ten Sefirot of the Upper Light and the Ten Sefirot of the Returning Light each and every one was necessarily composed of ten complete Sefirot. In like manner, in each and every secondary or tertiary Sefira there is complete interpenetration. There is nothing further to add here. See the *Inner Reflection* where the matter is explained at great length.

I[1]) That is to say every Upper Sefira encircles that below it equally on all sides, without any distinction of levels (see above, N).

CHAPTER 8

CLOSER AND FARTHER OF THE CIRCLES TO THE ENDLESS

Each and every circle in all the worlds in the void is superior or considered lofty in so far as it is closer (J¹) to or farther from the Light of the Endless. This earthly and material world is the Middle Point of all the circles in the void and empty air, and so it is farther than any other world is from the Endless. This explains why this world is so corporeal and material—indeed, it is the essence of corporeality: because it is the Middle Point of all the circles. Understand this well.

ח) כל עגול ועגול מכל העולמות כולם, אשר בתוך החלל, (י) כל הקרוב אל אור א״ס יותר מחברו, הוא עליון מאד ומשובח מחברו, עד שנמצא כי העולם הזה הארציי החומרי, הוא נקודה האמצעי תיכונה, תוך כל העגולים כולם, בתוך כל המקום החלל ואויר הפנוי הנ״ל. וגם הוא מרוחק מן הא״ס הרחקה גמורה, יותר מכל העולמות כולם. ועל כן הוא כל כך גשמי וחומרי בתכלית הגשמיות, עם היותו נקודה אמצעית בתוך כל העגולים, והבן זה היטב.

INNER LIGHT

J¹) We have already learned in discussing a related topic that space is not meant here, Heaven forbid. The meaning is rather nearness of form. We also know that from the Endless, PB''G, to the Middle Point there are four phases of change in form in the Ten Sefirot of the Circles, and that the Middle Point is the fourth phase, the impurest of all. The first Circle, called Crown, is the phase of the Root of these four phases, as said above. It goes without saying that the Circle of the Crown, the purest of all the Circles, is closer in form to the Endless than any of the others. Phase 1, slightly impurer than the Circle of the Crown is farther from the Endless, PB''G than this Circle. Phase 2, impurer or thicker than phase 1, is also farther from the Endless than is phase 1, and so on until the Middle Point, the thickest or impurest of all which is farther away from the Endless, PB''G than all others.

One may not contradict this argument with reference to volume 1, chapter 1, S which says that there is no phase of Above and Below in the Circles. For here we are referring to the period after the Circles have incorporated the illumination of the Line, at which time the distinction of above and below are introduced, along with all of the characteristics that inhere the line.

SECTION I

PART 2

Explaining the Ten Sefirot of Straightness, their emergence, their devolvement, and what they comprise (containing seven topical divisions):

Chapter 1

The order of emergence of the Ten Sefirot of Straightness.

Chapter 2

The five divisions of the soul of the Lower Man: Life, Spirit, Soul, Living, Individual.

Chapter 3

Both Circles and Straightness have Surrounding Light and Inner Light, and Outer Vessel and an Inner Vessel.

Chapter 4

The Light of the Circles is the Light of Life and the Light of Straightness is the Light of the Spirit. The Circles emanated before the Sefirot of Straightness.

Chapter 5

Arik Anpin of Circles illumines the Father and Mother of Circles through three windows it contains (right, left and center) from three Lines, and from them the Light is drawn to all of the Circles, so that all of the secondary emanations in Straightness are in Circles as well.

Chapter 6

Primordial Man was extended from the Endless to the very end of the World of Emanation, and it contains all of the Worlds—we are not permitted to deal with it.

Chapter 7

We are dealing in what follows with Straightness alone, not with Circles.

CHAPTER 1

EMERGENCE OF THE
TEN SEFIROT OF STRAIGHTNESS

And now we will explain the second phase of the ten sefirot, the phase of the Light of Straightness, resembling three lines in the form of the Upper Man. Just as the Line discussed above extends from above to below and the Circles emerge from its descent, so this Line too extends straightwise from above to below: from the upper roof (A) of the highest circle of all to the very bottom of the lowest circle of all, from top to bottom, comprising ten sefirot in the mystery (B) of the Image of the Straight Man of erect height (C) composed (D) of two hundred and forty eight limbs drawn in three lines, right, left and center, composed of ten primary sefirot, with each of these composed of ten secondary sefirot, and so on, ad infinitum.

א) ועתה נבאר בחינה הב׳ שיש ביוד ספירות, הלא הוא בחינת אור היושר, כדמיון ג׳ קוין, כצורת אדם העליון. והנה דרך הקו הנ״ל, המתפשט מלמעלה למטה, אשר ממנו מתפשטים העגולים, גם הקו ההוא מתפשט ביושר מל־ מעלה למטה, מראש (א) גג העל־ יון של עגול העליון מכולם, עד למטה מתחתית סיום כל העגולים ממש, מלמעלה למטה, כלול מיוד ספירות, בסוד (ב) צלם אדם ישר (ג) בעל קומה זקופה, (ד) כלול מרמ״ח אברים, מצטיירים בציור ג׳ קוים ימין ושמאל ואמצע, כלול מיוד ספירות בכללות, וכל ספירה וספירה מהם נפרטת ליוד ספירות, עד אין קץ.

INNER LIGHT

A) The Crown of a World or Sefira is the roof of that World or Sefira, and the Kingdom of a World of Sefira is the ground of that same World or Sefira. Thus the upper Circle is the Sefira of Crown, and its roof is the Crown of the Ten Sefirot of this Crown.

B) Levushe Hamochin are termed "form" or "likeness," from the root "Zel" meaning "shadow" or "shelter." Straight Illumination, composed of the first three Sefirot, is termed "Man," because it receives these 3 Sefirot as clothing—this is a lengthy matter, and this is not the time to go into it.

C) The head of every Sefira and Countenance is composed of the first three Sefirot: Crown, Wisdom, Intelligence. The seven lower Sefirot: Mercy, Judgement, Beauty, Lasting Endurance, Majesty, Foundation and Kingdom which are in every Sefira and Countenance are distinguished as the body of that Sefira and Countenance. When they are in order, in other words when the Light of the first three are in the Vessels of the first three and the Light of the seven lower are in the Vessels of the seven Lower then the Countenance is distinguished as "Of Upright Height." If, however, Lights of the body are found in the Vessels of the first three, instead of the appropriate Lights, then that countenance is distinguished as not being "Of Upright Height," for the phase of the Head is not more important than the phase of the Body, for even in the Head, Lights of the Body are to be found—this is called the Bowing of the Head, for the Head and the Body are at one level.

D) This means 248 phases of Mercy are in the Upper Countenance, from which are drawn 248 Limbs in the Lower Phases, as explained in the Mishnah Ohaloth. This is not the place to go into a lengthy explanation; more in the appropriate place.

CHAPTER 2

FIVE DIVISIONS OF
SOUL OF LOWER MAN

The Lower Man (E) has five different phases of Light: (F) Life, Spirit, Soul, Living, Individual. They are really (G) five degrees of Light, one above the other. This is the mystical meaning of reciting five times: "Let my soul praise God," as mentioned in the Talmudic Tractate Berachot, page ten, rect. ע"א. It stands for the five aspects of the soul.

ב) הנה יש (ה) באדם התחתון ה' בחינות אורות, שהם: (ו) הנפש, רוח, נשמה, חיה, יחידה. והם, (ז) ה' מעלות, זו למעלה מזו, וה"ס ה' פעמים ברכי נפשי את וכו', כנזכר במסכת ברכות (דף יוד ע"א), שהם, כנגד ה' בחינות שיש לנשמה.

INNER LIGHT

E) There is no Essence in all of the Worlds—whether in the Upper Worlds or in this World—which is not distinguished by the Ten Sefirot mentioned above: the four well known phases and their root. This is why Our Rabbi (Ari) writes that in the Lower Man in this World there are also found five phases etc.

F) The Vessels in the Ten Sefirot are called: Crown, Wisdom, Intelligence, Beauty, Kingdom. The Lights in these Ten

Sefirot are called: Individual, Living, Soul, Spirit, Life (as is written in Devarim Rabba, 2:26). The Light of the Individual is clothed in the Vessel of Crown, the Light of the Living is clothed in the Vessel of Wisdom, the Light of the Soul is clothed in the Vessel of Intelligence, the Light of the Spirit in the Vessel of Beauty and the Light of Life in the Vessel of Kingdom.

G) We already know that the distinction of levels is determined by the degree of purity or impurity and by everything "above" is meant the greater amount of purity.

CHAPTER 3

SURROUNDING AND INNER LIGHT, OUTER AND INNER VESSEL

The Ten Circular Sefirot all have the attributes mentioned above: (H) Lights and Vessels, (I) the Light being divided into Inner Light and Surrounding Light, (J) the Vessel being divided into Inner and Outer. The Ten Sefirot of Straightness, in the Image of a Man, also contain all of these attributes.

ג) והנה בחינת היוד ספירות העגולים כולם, יש בהם כל הבחינות הנ"ל, שהם: (ח) אורות וכלים, (ט) והאור נחלק, לאור פנימי, ואור מקיף, (י) והכלי נחלק, לחיצוניות ופנימיות. וכן בחינת יוד ספירות דיושר בציור אדם, יש בו כל הבחינות האלו בעצמם ג"כ.

INNER LIGHT

H) The Lights are NRNH''Y and the Vessels are KH''BZ''N mentioned above.

I) The reason for division of Spiritual Substance is the change in form which was undergone. (As mentioned above, volume 1, chapter 1, L, begin.: "But, etc.". "Higher than" means "purer than" while "lower than" means "impurer." For with the change in the form of its impurity, the substance separated and descended from its previous part, becoming

— 43 —

lower than it. To be sure, the Lights are influenced from Upper to Lower, on account of which the Lower must receive Abundance through its highest and purest phase, whereas the Upper gives Abundance through its lowest and impurest phases, whence the equivalence between the Light from Upper Light and the form of the Vessel of the Lower, for the impurer and coarser phase of the Upper is equivalent to the finer and purer phase of the Lower. It turns out that the Lower is unable to receive all of the Light it is supposed to receive, receiving merely a small part of it, i.e. only as much as its purest Vessel can receive. Its other phases being not as pure, must remain without the Light related to them because of the change in their form over and against the Upper which influences them.

Therefore we have distinguished here that the Light belonging to the Lower divides into two phases: the first is the small measure of Light which it receives from the Upper in its uppermost Vessel, as explained above, this Light being called "The Inner Light" in the Lower. The second is the entire measure of Light belonging to the phases remaining in the Lower, unable to receive from the Upper because of their change of form (as explained above); the entire measure is distinguished because it remained in the Upper, not descending to the Lower, and is called "Surrounding Light." This is its name because it surrounds the Lower—illuminating it from a distance, even though not clothed in it; this constitutes diminished illumination, at a distance. This distant illumination tends to purify the impure phases in the Lower, until the equivalence of forms of all the Lower phases with the form of the Upper is expected—at which time it can receive all the Light appropriate to it. This is termed the "Incorporation of the Surrounding Lights"; in other words: the Surrounding Lights have been incorporated, becoming clothed in the Vessels of the Lower and purified to the point of becoming phases of Inner Light.

J) In other words: because the Lights were divided into Inner Light and Surrounding Light (as explained above) two types of Receival in the Vessel are to be found—Receival into the Vessel and Receival exterior to the Vessel (See the *Table of Answers*, volume 1, 102)—whereby the Inner Light is received *into* the Vessel and the Surrounding Light which purified its impurity (as explained above) is received through the exterior of the Vessel, in other words without being clothed in the Vessel.

The division into exterior and interior with respect to the Vessel depends on the distinction of purity or impurity in the Vessel, for only the impurity of the Vessel is worthy to receive the Inner Light, since the essence of the Vessel of Receival of the Emanation is phase four. However, the first three phases are not worthy of Receival but rather cause the revelation of the fourth phase. Thus every Vessel is in itself distinguished into the four phases in the Vessel with the Light mainly being received in the fourth phase, therefore called the Interior of the Vessel, where the Abundance resides.

The three phases which cause the revelation of the fourth phase in the Vessel, they themselves not being agents of Receival, are considered as encircling the exterior of the fourth phase. Compare the four layers of wood of an actual material vessel, each layer with in the next—anything placed in the Vessel is in its interior, this being the innermost layer, the other three layers merely strengthening the inner one, enabling it to support what is placed in it. Similarly, with respect to Spiritual Substance, the phase which holds the Abundance is the fourth phase of the Vessel, the first three phases are the causes which reveal the fourth in all its power to the point where it is capable of holding the Abundance, but they themselves are not agents of Receival for the Inner Light.

Therefore they are called Exterior of the Vessel, since they are exterior to the phase of Receival of the Inner Light: phase 3 being exterior to phase 4, phase 2 being exterior to phase 3, and phase one being most exterior of all, surrounding all. All of them also have an exterior phase without any impurity whatsoever, this being the phase of the Root of all four phases in the Vessel. One should be aware of the fact that this perfectly pure phase is the Vessel of Receival for the Surrounding Light, for on account of its miraculous purity it is able to receive the illumination of the Surrounding Light, even though it is at a distance.

As for the division of the Vessel: its Interior means the impurest phase in the Vessel, that is to say the fourth phase in the Vessel which receives the Inner Light; its Exterior means the purest phase in the Vessel, that is to say the phase of the Root of the Vessel (as said above) which receives the Surrounding Light from a distance. One may not pose the question that the fourth phase is not capable of Receival because of the Restriction and the Curtain; for we are dealing here merely with the phase of Returning Light which ascends from the fourth phase (See the *Inner Reflection*).

CHAPTER 4

THE LIGHT OF
CIRCLES AND STRAIGHTNESS

However, the difference between Circles and Straightness is that (K) the Ten Circular Sefirot are composed of the Light of Life, and they contain an Inner Light and a Surrounding Light, one within and the other without. They have, moreover, ten sefirot of vessels, each vessel having an interior and an exterior. Furthermore they have ten sefirot of Light, each Light containing an Inner Light and Surrounding Light. But the Ten Sefirot of Straightness are composed of the Light called (L) Spirit, a higher degree of Light than the Light of Life, as is known. They too are composed of an Inner Light and a Surrounding Light, and they also possess ten sefirot of Vessels, each vessel having an interior and an exterior. It goes almost without saying that the phase

ד) אמנם, החילוק שיש בין העגו־
לים להיושר, הוא, כי (כ) י"ס
דעגולים הם בחינת האור הנקרא
נפש, ויש בהם אור פנימי ואור
מקיף, פנימי וחיצון: שיש לה
בחינת יוד ספירות של כלים, ובכל
כלי מהם יש פנימיות וחיצוניות,
וגם יש יוד ספירות של אורות,
לכל אור יש בו אור פנימי ואור
מקיף. אבל הי"ס דיושר, הם בחי־
נת האור הנקרא (ל) רוח, שהוא
מדרגה גבוה על מדרגת הנפש,
כנודע, גם הם כלולים מאו"פ
ואו"מ, גם יש להם, יוד ספירות
דכלים, ובכל כלי מהם יש בו
פנימיות וחיצוניות. ופשיטא היא
שבחינת הנפש נאצלה תחילה, ו־
אח"כ נאצל הרוח.

of Life was emanated first,
then came the phase of Spirit.

INNER LIGHT

K) The Light in all of the Sefirot which are only able to receive Lights but are unable to influence others is termed Light of Life, and we have already explained that all of the Light in the Circles must be received from the Light of the Line (as explained above, chapter 1, L). The reason is that it is impossible for the Upper Light to be bound to the Vessels by any other means than intercourse with the Curtain which sends up the Returning Light which (the Returning Light) binds the Upper Light to the Vessels, as will be explained (Inner Reflection, chapter 7, 79). Therefore the Upper Light is unable to bind with Vessels lacking this Curtain, which would enable them to influence others, from above to below; they are only capable of receiving Light from the preceding level, from below to above, for the purpose of their existence alone, this Light being called Light of Life, as said above. Therefore, since there is no Curtain in the Vessels of Circles, as said above, the Upper Light does not bind with them directly, instead they must receive the Light from the Line, and only enough for their existence, not enough to influence others, as explained. This is why the Light in the Circles is called Light of Life, as explained.

L) The Ten Sefirot of Spirit are phases which influence, therefore the Light of the Spirit is called the Male Light, since it influences. But the Ten Sefirot of Life are termed Female Light, receiving without being able to influence. This is why the Ten Sefirot of the Light of the Line are termed Ten Sefirot of Spirit, to indicate that they are a male phase of Light which influences; the reason for this has been explained above. Thus the Level of Spirit is higher than the level of Life, since it influences it.

CHAPTER 5

LONG FACE ILLUMINES
FATHER AND MOTHER OF CIRCLES

Even though the (M) Ten Circular Sefirot are concentric they still (N) possess all the phases of receival of Abundance that the Ten Sefirot of the Line of Straightness possess. The reason for this is that the Circular Crown (called, (O) after the emendation, "Long Face"), has (P) a single breach and an aperture or window on the (Q) right side of the Circle from which its Light (R) descends to the Circle of Father and illumines it. There is a second window on the left side of the Circle of the Long Face from which the Light descends to the left side of the Circle of Father and (S) penetrates it, forming a window through which the Light is drawn to the Circle of Mother within the Circle of Father and il-

* ה) גם בהיות היוד ספירות בב־
חינת (מ) עגולים, זה בתוך זה, יש
(נ) בהם כל הבחינות של קבלת
השפע, שביוד ספירות שבקו היו־
שר, והוא, כי בעגול הכתר, הנקרא
(ס) אריך אנפין אחר התיקון, יש
(ע) נקב אחד וחלון (פ) בצד ימין
העגול, ומשם (צ) יורד אור אריך
אל עגול אבא, ומאיר אליו. ועוד
יש חלון שני, בשמאל העגול של
אריך, ויוצא האור עד צד שמאל
דעגול אבא, אשר בתוכו, (ק) ונוק־
בו ונעשה בו חלון, ומשם נמשך
האור עד עגול אמא, שבתוך עגול
אבא, ומאיר בו. ונמצא כי בעבור
האור תוך שמאל עגול אבא, אינו
לאבא עצמו, ואינו (ר) עובר שם
רק דרך מעבר בלבד, אבל עי־
קר הארה היא לאמא. ונמצא כי
א״א, מאיר לאבא ואמא יחד, כמו
שהוא בענין היושר שלהם ממש.

* Shaar Hakdamot, page 11 (Jerusalem ed)   * שער הקדמות דף י״א (דפוס ירושלם).

— 50 —

lumines it. *We find that the
Light from the left of the Circle of Father does not really
belong to the Circle of Father,
but merely (T) passes through
it, its real purpose being to
illumine the Circle of Mother.
Thus the Long Face illumines
Father and Mother together,
as is the case with their Sefirot of Straightness. And even
though they are concentric circles they possess (U) Straight
Lines: Right, Left, and Center, in their windows. From
there the Light is drawn to
the Ten Circular Sefirot by
Straight Lines, and so all of
the secondary sefirot in the
Ten Sefirot of the Straight
Line of Spirit as well.**

ואף כי הם עגולים זו בתוך זו,
יש להם (ש) קוים ישרים: ימין,
ושמאל, ואמצע, בבחינת החלונות
האלו שבהם. ומשם, נמשך האור
ביוד ספירות דעגולים, דרך קוים
ישרים ממש, בכל הפרטים עצמם
כולם, אשר ביוד ספירות דקו ישר
דרוח, ממש.

INNER LIGHT

M) In other words, the five levels KH''BZ''N (Crown,
Wisdom, Intelligence, Beauty and Kingdom) are not extended
straightwise, meaning one beneath the other, from pure to impure (volume 2, part 2, E), instead they are equivalent to one
another, without one being lower—that is, impurer than the
other. Nevertheless there is, to be sure, the distinction between
them of cause and effect since one comes out of the other

and one is extended from another—Wisdom coming from the Crown, Intelligence from Wisdom, Beauty from Intelligence, and the Kingdom from the Beauty (as explained above, in the *Inner Light*, volume 1, part 1, N, begin.: "Now...").

This distinction of cause and effect is defined by their being found one inside the other, each cause encircling its effect: Wisdom encircled by Crown, Intelligence encircled by Wisdom, etc. Thus "one inside the other" means one encircled by the other, as explained. But there is no distinction whatsoever of above and below between them (as explained above, volume 1, part 1, S).

N) Thus the Light is impressed by the Vessel in which it is clothed, so that even when it goes out to another Vessel it does not change its course from what it was in the previous Vessel. Therefore, since while the Light was still in the Line of Straightness it was drawn and descended lower and lower (i.e., it became impurer from level to level because of the Curtain found there) (as explained above, volume 2, part 1, F), for this reason, even after it has emerged and come to the Ten Sefirot of Circles which do not have a Curtain and has circled in them, nevertheless it does not change its course in its extension from level to level. This means, for example, when the Light of the Line comes to the Sefira of the Crown it circles i.e., it takes on the shape of that Vessel, since there is no distinction of above and below; however, when the Light extends from the Circle of the Crown to the Circle of Wisdom it does not become circular (see the *Table of Answers*, volume 1, 3), but instead is drawn straightwise, i.e. with a distinction of above and below. This is why the Circular Sefira of Wisdom is found below the Circle of the Crown, and is impurer than the Crown, their forms not being equivalent. Similarly, when the Light comes from Wisdom to Intelligence it is drawn to it straightwise. Intelligence is distinguished by being lower than Wisdom, that is to say impurer than Wisdom. Similarly with all the Sefirot. Even though the Ten Circular Sefirot are equivalent in form without the distinction of above and below with respect to Vessels, (as explained above), still there *is* the distinction of above and below with respect to: "They still possess all the phases of receival of Abundance that the Ten Sefirot of the Line of Straightness possess." (See Ari text, volume 2, part 2, chapter 5).

O) This means that after the Restoration of the four worlds: Emanation, Creation, Formation, and Action, each Sefira became a whole Countenance in Head, Middle and End. Because of this they received different names. The Countenance made from the Crown is called the Long Face. The Countenance made from Wisdom is called Father. The Countenance made from Intelligence is called Mother. The Countenance made from the six Sefirot: HG"TNH"Y (Chesed, G'vurah, Tiferet, Netzach, Hod and Yesod) is called Small Face. The Countenance made from Kingdom is called Nukvah. The meanings of these names will be explained in the proper place, with God's help.

P) This means, as we already know, that because of the Light of the Ten Sefirot of the Line which is received in the Circles all of the phases of Straightness are necessarily impressed on the Circles as well (as explained above, N, begin.: "There are..."). Thus the phase in the Returning Light of the Line called Curtain which binds the Upper Light in the Vessels (as explained above, volume 2, part 1, K), this Curtain makes an impression on the Circles, but without its impurity, since this impurity could not by any means ascend from a lower level to a higher one, since the very meaning of "higher," is not having any impurity such as is to be found in the lower level—one must understand this. It is only the concept of the benefits which this Curtain reveals in the Lower of the Ten Sefirot of Straightness, this alone ascending from the Curtain of the Line of Straightness and impressing the Circles. The benefit from this Curtain is termed "Window," similar to a window placed in a room to bring light into it: so this Curtain reveals the Returning Light in all its value to bind the Light to the Emanation. If the Curtain were to disappear then the Light would withdraw from the Emanation leaving it in darkness, as would happen if the window in a room were sealed over. Thus when we wish to refer only to the benefit of the Curtain we define it as "a window or aperture."

Q) That is to say it also impresses both right and left which served the Ten Sefirot of Straightness (see the *Table of Answers* volume 1, 23).

R) In other words, because of this window the distinction of drawing and descent of the Light was made possible, whereby the Light is impurified from level to level, the lower level being impurer than the one above it. Thus it is written: "From which its Light descends to the Circle of Father." In other words, because of the window the Light receives the attributes of impurity and downwardness with respect to the Father of

Circles, which is Wisdom, having been lowered one level, no longer being equivalent to the Crown of the Circles, as it was before it received the Light of Straightness through the window. Similarly with Intelligence which is lower than Wisdom.

S) This teaches us that the window is made in the Sefirot along with the descent of the Light upon it from the Upper Circle. In other words, it is then that the Light impresses upon it the Curtain it contains, as explained above. Thus it is to be distinguished as if the Light pierces it and makes a window in it.

T) This matter has already been well explained above (volume 2, part 1, D[1]).

U) In other words, the Light descends from Circle to Circle drawn straightwise, in straight lines, but this is not considered the actual phase of the Restoration of Lines descending from the "Curtain" containing the Male Light, and thus able to influence others. Instead, these Lines of the Circles do not have the power of Influence since they descend through "Windows" sufficient only to receive the Light necessary for themselves alone, not enough to influence others. The general rule is: anything without the phase of the Curtain does not have Male Light, but rather Female Light, which is Light of Life.

CHAPTER 6

PRIMORDIAL MAN

*The (V) Primordial Man (A¹) spans the entire void of emanation referred to above, from its upper to its lower extremities. In this Man are included all of the Worlds, as, with God's help, was explained above. But regarding (B¹) the inner form and essence of this Man we are not at all permitted to speak.**

* ו) והנה (ת) האִ״ק הזה, (א) מב־ריח מן הקצה אל הקצה, מן קצה העליון עד קצה התחתון, בכל חלל האצילות הנ״ל. ובזה האדם נכללין כל העולמות כמ״ש בע״ה, אבל, (ב) בבחינת פנימית ועצמותו של אדם זה, אין לנו רשות לדבר בו ולהתעסק כלל.

INNER LIGHT

V) One should not marvel at the use of the term "Man" here. It resembles the saying of Rabbi Yodan (Midrash Rabba, Genesis 27): "The power of the prophets is great, for they compare creature to creator, as it is written 'I heard the voice of a man amongst... etc. and on the image of the chair the image of a man on it'." The reason for this will be explained in its place, with God's help.

* Tree of life Sate 1.

* ע״ח שער א' ענף ב'.

A¹) This means from the Endless, PB''G, the purest of all the Worlds until the Middle Point which is the most impure phase of all the worlds. Thus all of Reality before us, things above and below, are all branches which have devolved from the Endless and are suspended from the Endless; and clothe the Endless, and the Endless binds them all together.

B¹) The interior refers to the phase of the Light of the Endless clothed in it; its essence is the phases of its first three Sefirot. It has already been explained (Introduction, 27, begin.: *Additionally) that we have no right to speak at all about the phases of the first three Sefirot at each level and Countenance, even in the World of Action. However the phases of the seven lower Sefirot we may deal with, even the seven lower Sefirot of the first three Sefirot of Primordial Man. (N.B.)

CHAPTER 7

VESSELS OF STRAIGHTNESS
FOLLOW CIRCLES

First (C¹) to emerge were the Ten Circular Sefirot, one within the other, and afterwards the Image of a Man (D¹) was drawn straightwise in these Circles across their whole length. But our subject is the phase of Straightness, not (E¹) the phase of Circles.

ז) אמנם (ג) בתחילה יצאו יוד ספירות דרך עגול, אלו תוך אלו, ואחר כך בתוך העגולים, נמשך דרך יושר כציור אדם אחד, (ד) באורך כל העגולים הנזכרים לעיל, (ה) ואין אנו עוסקים כלל בבחינת עגולים, רק בבחינת יושר לבד.

INNER LIGHT

C¹) It has already been explained above that the Circles were revealed at once with the Restriction and Withdrawal of the Light, and that afterwards Straightness was revealed by distinguishing the Circles into cause and effect of the Light of the Line, which is the way they are distinguished from those that precede them. (As is written in the *Table of Answers*, this section, 42).

D¹) This means from the Upper edge to the lower edge, as explained above. If we study the analagous material situation we can understand its Spiritual root. In the analagous material situation we may understand that there are three distinctions: the upper edge, the lower edge, the distance between them. In the same way we may distinguish the spiritual dimension: first there is the lowest edge of the level, which is the last and impurest phase, with no phase impurer below it, which teaches us at once about the upper edge, for the extent of impurity in the last phase determines the height of the Returning Light (N.B. The *Inner Reflection*, 86a, begin.: "It has been thoroughly explained..."). For example, the impurity of phase four in phase four reaches the height of the Crown in the Crown, and the impurity of phase three in phase four reaches only to the Crown of Wisdom, and phase two in phase four reaches only to the height of the Crown in Intelligence, etc. Thus if the Lower edge is determined, the upper edge is thereby also determined. After the two edges in the level are determined the distance between them is determined at once, for Spiritual distance means the change in form between two phases, the extent of change determining the distance. For example, if the lower edge is phase one of phase four, then the upper edge is only at the height of the Crown of Beauty (read thoroughly the section in the *Inner Reflection* referred to above), the distance not being very far. But if the lower edge is phase two, then the upper edge is at the height of the Crown of Intelligence; thus the distance between them is two phases of impurity, phase one and two. If its lower edge is the impurity of phase 3 of phase 4, then the upper edge is the Crown of Wisdom; in this case the distance is three phases, and so on, in like manner. Understand this well.

E[1]) This is because the Circles cause the phase of the first three Sefirot of Straightness (As explained above, volume 2, part 1, R, begin.: "The reason for this..."). With respect to their Vessels, they are immeasurably superior to the first three Sefirot of Straightness, as explained above. We already know that it is not permitted to speak of or treat the first three Sefirot, thus we have no right to treat any phases of Circles.

SECTION II

INNER REFLECTION

Chapter 1
The Ten Sefirot of Circles.

Chapter 2
Primordial and ABY"A.

Chapter 3
Essence and Material of the Vessels.

Chapter 4
Four Aspects of Impurity.

Chapter 5
Restriction and the Curtain.

Chapter 6
The Curtain and the Returning Light.

Chapter 7
Purification and Emergence of the Five Levels.

Chapter 8
Drawing and Clothing of the Vessels.

Chapter 9
Primary, Secondary and Tertiary Sefirot.

Chapter 10
Binding by Striking.

CHAPTER 1

THE TEN SEFIROT OF CIRCLES

Explaining: The Ten Sefirot of Circles, in 6 topics:

1. The Circles are the phase of the first three Sefirot.

2. In Sefirot of Circles, every outer Sefira is more important; the opposite is the case with Sefirot of Straightness, the inner Sefira being more important.

3. The 2 phases of receival in the Vessels:
   a) through their interior.
   b) through their exterior.

4. The 4th phase cannot be revealed except by means of the 3 phases which precede and induce its revelation.

5. The 4 phases are like 4 layers, one on top of the other in Layered Vessel, the Abundance being received in the innermost layer.

6. Every thicker Curtain sends the Returning Light higher up than a less thick one; there are 5 heights to which the Returning Light is sent up.

1) Our Rabbi (Ari) says very little about the Ten Circular Sefirot, and even the few things he says are apparently full of contradictions—but it is impossible to say any more about them, because they are a phase of the first three Sefirot with

which we are not permitted to deal; however, those few things which Our Rabbi (Ari) has written must be explained nonetheless in great detail and with great precision, sufficient to Our Rabbi's (Ari) purpose, which is to say, as much as is required for a coherent understanding of the Wisdom of the Kabbalah.

2) First let us understand his general conception: he divides all of existence into 2 phases: Circles and Straightness; in other words, all of the Countenances in the 5 worlds: Primordial Man and ABY"A, up until this world, have 10 Sefirot of Circles and 10 Sefirot of Straightness. We have seen that with respect to Sefirot of Circles, every more exterior sefira is superior and every more interior sefira is inferior, because the highest Circle closest to the Endless which circles and surrounds all existence, is called Crown, within it is the second Circle called Wisdom, inferior to Crown, and so on—until the innermost sphere—this world, the most inferior of all the Circles, dark, without Light, full of filth. Thus, every interior circle is inferior and every exterior circle is superior.

3) The opposite holds true for the Sefirot of Straightness, the interior Sefira in this case being superior, since with respect to the Ten Sefirot of Straightness, the first and most interior Sefirot are Ten Sefirot of the World of Primordial Man, termed the Line, which extend from the Endless drawn close to this world but not touching it. Exterior to it and clothing it are the Ten Sefirot of Straightness of the second World, called the World of Emanation descended from the World of Primordial Man. Exterior to the World of Emanation and clothing it are Ten Sefirot of Straightness of the

World of Creation, inferior to Emanation, and so on, until the Ten Sefirot of Straightness of the World of Action, the most inferior of all, which is exterior to and clothes all the worlds. Thus, with respect to the Sefirot of Straightness we find that every exterior Sefira is inferior, and every interior Sefira is superior. This is opposite of what holds true for the Ten Sefirot of the Circles, as explained above. Thus there is a vast and profound difference between the Sefirot of Circles and the Sefirot of Straightness—one must understand it very well.

4) We already know about the Middle Point in the End-less, PB''G, where the Restriction took place, with the Light removing from the surrounding of the Point and causing an empty void (See above, volume 1, part 1, 50, begin.: "And this fourth phase"). It was explained above that this is why Middle Point is its name, to indicate that it does not receive through its interior, but from its surrounding exterior, thereby receiving Light without restricted measure, since whatever receives from its exterior makes no bounds to the Light received (see the above, closely). Thus there are two modes of receival in the Vessels: the first is receival from the exterior, the second is receival from the interior. Of course this does not refer to place and extent, which "interior" and "exterior" would seem to suggest. Thus we must understand well what kind of interior and exterior we are dealing with here.

5) The Spiritual Vessel, we already know, is a matter of a phase of "Desire," in the Emanation, to receive its Abundance from the Endless (See *Table of Answers*, volume 1, 25). We also know that this Desire has 4 phases, one below the other,

in other words, this vessel (the aforementioned "Desire to Receive") is not fixed in the Emanation ready to perform its function until 4 phases pass over it in order—the 1st phase is a very weak Desire, the 2nd a large one, and so on, until the 4th phase, which is a Desire large enough to fix and complete the Vessel. The reason for this has already been explained above (volume 1, part 1, letter N begin.: „And the reason") to which the reader is referred. Since this Desire to Receive is antithetical to the Desire to Influence (Bestow) in the Light of the Endless, PB"G, it is unable to be revealed all at once, but must emerge slowly: first from the Desire to Influence (Bestow) in the Root, called Crown, then to phase 1, somewhat changed, more impure, then phase 2, still more impure, and so on, until the 4th phase, which is diametrically opposite to the Light, and is fit to serve as a Vessel in the Emanation—which is not the case with the preceding 3 phases, in which the Desire to Receive is not sufficiently revealed to serve as a Vessel of Receival, thus only the 4th phase is considered the major part of the Vessel of Receival in the Emanation, being called on this account the interior phase of the Emanation, however, phase 3 in the Desire to Receive is exterior to the 4th phase, phase 2 exterior to phase 3, and phase 1 exterior to phase 2, the Crown being exterior to all. Compare the walls of a material Vessel made of 4 layers, one on top of the other, the Abundance received in this Vessel is surely at the 4th innermost level alone, the three exterior, surrounding levels made to strengthen the innermost 4th level. Thus we judge here that the Light is received in the 4th phase alone, the 3 preceding levels being exterior to it and coming into existence only because the 4th phase can only be revealed by means of the devolvement explained above.

6) The distinction of the interior and exterior of a Vessel has been well explained, since there must be 4 phases in each Vessel, thus the last of these phases is called the inside and interior of the Vessel, since it is the major phase of receival in the Vessel; the phases which preceded it in order to reveal the last phase are distinguished as the exterior of the Vessel. Every level farther away from the last phase is considered more exterior. We also know that phase 1 is purer than phase 2, and phase 4 is the impurest of all—thus interiority and impurity are one and the same, and the fact that the 4th phase is considered the phase which receives the abundance is only because it is more impure. Exteriority and purity are one and the same, since its Desire is weak and pure, closer to the Emanating phase—thus more exterior, which is to say farther from being a phase of receival, which would mean interiority.

7) This is why Our Rabbi (Ari) writes with respect to Sefirot of Circles that the more exterior is superior, and closer to the Emanator, since the Root, called Crown, is the purest of all, most similar of all in form to the Endless, PB''G, which means closer to the Emanator, which means most exterior—which is to say furthest from the phase of interiority, the phase of receival discussed above. Next comes phase 1, more interior than the Crown, which is to say closer to the phase of receival than is the Crown. Phase 2 is more interior than phase 1, closer to the 4th phase, which is the phase of receival—the 4th phase being the true interior since it receives the Abundance, and so its form is farthest from the Emanator, as explained above.

8) However, with Sefirot of Straightness there is the matter of the Returning Light which ascends from the juncture (intercourse) of the curtain with the Upper Light (see volume 1, *Table of Answers*, *s.v.* "curtain"), its size being measured by the amount of impurity in the Curtain which joins with the Upper Light—so that the most impure Curtain, the 4th phase, sends up the entire height of Ten Sefirot, up to the Crown. If, however, the amount of impurity in the Curtain is less by one phase, having only the 3rd phase, then ten Sefirot are sent up, each reaching only the height of Wisdom, each lacking the Crown; if the amount of impurity is only that of the 2nd phase, then ten Sefirot are sent up each reaching only to the height of Intelligence, each lacking Crown and Wisdom. If the Curtain has only the impurity of phase 1 then it sends up ten Sefirot, each reaching only to the height of the Small Face—and if the Curtain is pure, having not even the impurity of phase 1, then no height is sent up, only the phase of Kingdom. The reason for this will be explained in volume 3, with God's help.

CHAPTER 2

PRIMORDIAL AND ABY''A

Explaining: The 5 major distinctions between the 5 worlds: P''M, and ABY''A in 6 topics:

1. The 5 worlds called P''M, ABY''A distinguished by the 4 phases of impurity in the Curtain.
2. The Upper influences the lower only if it is impurer. The lower receives from the Upper only when it is purer.
3. The reason for the disappearance of the Light from the 3 phases preceding the 4th phase, when only the 4th phase was Restricted.
4. The explanation of binding (Intercourse) through Striking.
5. What the Returning Light is which ascends from below to above by means of Binding (Intercourse) through Striking.
6. The Returning Light which ascends from Binding (Intercourse) through Striking becomes a Vessel of Receival for the Upper Light in place of the 4th phase.

9) Know that the 5 worlds, P''M and ABY''A of Straightness are distinguished in the main, by the amount of impurity found in the Curtain of their Vessels; because a Curtain in the Vessels of the World of Primordial Man is very impure, the impurity of the 4th phase, there being no greater impurity

in all the worlds, therefore its ten Sefirot are complete, which is to say each one reaches the height of Crown, close to the Light of the Endless, PB"G. This is the first and most important world of all from the Light of the Endless, PB"G, to this World. Thus it is distinguished as standing as the most interior of the Worlds, since interiority and impurity are one and the same, and since the Curtain in the Vessels of Primordial Man is the 4th phase—the impurest of all phases—thus it is most interior.

10) The Curtain in the Vessels of the World of Emanation is not as impure as the Curtain in the World of Primordial Man, since its impurity is only the 3rd phase; therefore the ten Sefirot of Straightness of Emanation do not reach a height higher than the height of Wisdom, lacking Crown, and thereby considered lower with respect to the Sefirot of Crown in the World of Primordial Man. They are distinguished as exterior to the ten Sefirot of Primordial Man, since the impurity of the 3rd phase is exterior to the impurity of the 4th phase, exteriority and purity being one and the same, as explained above. Thus, the World of Emanation clothes—i.e. is exterior to the World of Primordial Man, the more interior of the two.

11) The Curtain in the Vessels of the ten Sefirot of the World of Creation is more pure than the Curtain in the World of Emanation, having only the impurity of phase 2, thus the height of these ten Sefirot is not greater than Intelligence, and so the world of Creation is considered more exterior than the World of Emanation which has impurity of phase 3, making it more interior than the World of Creation, having only the impurity of phase 2. Thus the World of Creation is distinguished as exterior to and clothing the World of Emanation.

12) The Curtain in the World of Formation has only the impurity of phase 1, the weakest of all, thus the ten Sefirot in the World of Formation are of short height, reaching only to the level of the Small Face, lacking the first 3 Sefirot: Crown, Wisdom, and Intelligence. Thus the World of Formation is exterior to the World of Creation which has impurity of phase 2, which is interior to phase 1 in the World of Formation, as explained above; thus the World of Formation is distinguished as exterior to and clothing the World of Creation.

13) The Curtain in the Ten Sefirot of Straightness in the World of Action is perfectly pure, without any impurity whatsoever, thus there is no juncture (Intercourse) with the Upper Light, sending up a Returning Light. Since they do not have a Returning Light they also do not have the Upper Light, since the Upper Light is not fixed in the Countenance without Returning Light. Thus these ten Sefirot have only a height reaching Kingdom alone, lacking the first 9 Sefirot: Crown, Wisdom, Intelligence, and the Small Face (comprised of 6 Sefirot: HG"T, NH"Y). Because their Curtain is the purest amongst all the preceding Worlds they are thereby distinguished as most exterior of all. We already know that purity and exteriority are one and the same, as explained above. Thus the World of Formation whose Vessels have a Curtain of phase 1 is nevertheless considered an interior World with respect to the World of Action. The World of Action is distinguished as exterior to and clothing the World of Formation, as well as all the other worlds, since it is the purest of all.

14) One should not marvel because reason suggests the most important Light ought to be clothed in the purest Ves-

sels, since a pure Vessel's form is closer to the Light—and
how is it said here that the impure is higher? However, we
must understand that the clothing of the Light in the Vessels
is a separate matter, and the Influence of the Upper Light on
the Countenance is a separate matter—the two are far apart,
indeed they are of antithetical value. The rule is: the Upper
doesn't influence the Lower unless it is thicker or impurer,
and the Lower does not receive Light from the Upper unless
it is purer. One must understand this well, since it is an important key in Kabbalistic Wisdom.

15) To understanding this we must understand more about
Restriction and Line; we know that the Restriction occured
only in phase 4, termed Kingdom of the Endless, PB"G, or
the Middle Point.—The reason for this is simple. Since the
meaning of Restriction is a matter of preventing the Desire to
Receive, which is to say stopping itself from receiving Abundance from the Light of the Endless, and since the only Vessel
of Receival is phase 4 alone, thus the Restriction falls only
on phase 4. It has already been explained above that the 3
phases which preceded the 4th phase are not at all considered
Vessels of receival, only causers of receival, since by their
devolvement the Vessel of receival is revealed—the 4th phase.
Thus the Restriction does not fall on them at all, but only
on the Middle Point, which is the 4th phase—as explained.

16) Therefore, since the Desire of the 4th phase to Receive
was diminished, the Light withdrew from the 3 preceding
phases as well, since they contain no other Vessels of Receival
which might hold the Light, and even the Lights belonging
to the 3 preceding phases must be received in the 4th phase

(since they do not have their own Vessels of receival, as explained above), thus when the Light ceased to be received in phase 4 all of the Light disappeared at once.

17) After the withdrawal of the Light on account of the Restriction, Light was drawn again from the Endless, PB''G, in the form of the Line, which is a small quantity of Light possessing only the first 3 phases of the Desire to Receive, without the 4th phase (as explained above); (N.B. volume 1, part 2, B, begin.: "And was drawn etc."). From what has been explained, (that there is no Vessel of Receival in the 1st three phases of Desire whatsoever), one might ask: How can Light be received without Vessels of Receival, since these 3 phases do not have, as yet, a phase of receival, whereas phase 4, which is alone a Vessel of Receival for the Countenance is not present in the phase of the Line?

18) The answer is that since the effect of the Restriction is on the Emanation, and not at all on the Emanator, therefore the Upper Light is not cut off from the Restriction of the Middle Point, and so the Upper Light descends to the 4th phase as well, but the 4th phase prevents it from entering it, because of the preceding Restriction effecting phase 4 before the arrival of this Light. This is what is termed in the literature as "Binding (Intercourse) by Striking," which resembles what happens when two objects, the one wanting to pass over and break through the fence and boundary of the second, the second object resisting with all its strength, preventing the first object from achieving its goal, each object thus pushing against the other. The resemblance is to two hard objects— since the nature of liquids allows mixing and interpenetra-

tion, as does a soft object, which also allows slight inter-penetration at the outer layers—but this is not the case with two hard objects, where one does not allow the other to push it from its boundaries, and so two hard objects which meet strike one another, the meeting itself making the striking—in this manner we are to understand the spreading of the Upper Light from the Endless, PB"G, which fills the 4th phase as well with namely that quantity of the Endless, PB"G, in the form of the Light that descends to be clothed in phase 4, but the power of Restriction in phase 4 prevents it, not allow-ing the Straight Light to enter it. Thus we understand this meeting of the Upper Light and the Power of Restriction as "Binding (Intercourse) by Striking," which is to say that each disturbs and hinders the path and tendency of the other, since the Light of the Endless tends naturally to fill phase 4, and phase 4 tends naturally to push the Upper Light away and not receive it, as explained.

19) From the meeting and striking in the 4th phase dis-cussed above, a new Light is born and emerges; compare the Light of the sun when it strikes a mirror, (a piece of glass colored on one side), so that the sunbeans cannot pass through the mirror but instead are reflected back, sending brightness away from the mirror's surface. This is what happens when the Upper Light strikes the Power of Restriction in the 4th phase, termed "Curtain"; the Curtain returns the Light to its Root. However, this is not a matter of disappearance of Light—quite the opposite: the returning of the Upper Light from the 4th phase upwards constitutes a distinctly new Light which ascends to the Upper Light, and clothes it. Thus it is

distinguished as a phase of a Vessel which receives the Upper Light.

20) We must keep in mind that the phase of the Head of each Countenance has no other Vessels of Receival other than the Returning Light, as will be explained in the proper place. All the power of Receival in this Returning Light is due to the birth and emergence from the phase of striking in the 4th phase, as explained above—because it is born from phase 4 it becomes a Vessel of Receival like phase 4. This matter will be fully explained in the 3rd lesson, its appropriate place.

21) Now one can understand the question raised above: How can the Upper Light spread only in 3 phases, which do not have, as yet, Vessels of Receival? (See above). From what has been explained one can well understand that the phase of Receival of the Upper Light still flows only from the 4th phase, but in the phase of the Vessel of Receival of the Returning Light which ascends from Binding (Intercourse) by Striking in the 4th phase, and this Returning Light is a phase of a Vessel of Receival found in the Line drawn from the Endless, PB''G, into the void, and it is exactly like the 4th phase itself, because it is a phase of Receival in the Endless, PB''G. Thus, now that after the Restriction the 4th phase is lacking, the Returning Light, born by means of the Curtain in the 4th phase, takes the 4th phase's place—understand this well.

22) It has been thoroughly explained that even though there are 4 phases in the Desire to Receive, nevertheless not all of the phases are considered Vessels of Receival, merely the 4th phase. It has also been explained that the Vessel of Receival of the Line, drawn from the Endless, PB''G, to the Void, after

the Restriction, is the phase of the Returning Light which ascends from the Curtain in the 4th phase. Since it was born from the 4th phase it was empowered by the 4th phase as a Vessel of Receival. It will be explained in the proper place that this Returning Light is not completely sufficient for the task of Receival until it also spreads from the Curtain downwards, whereby the Curtain spreads again to 4 levels, until the 4th phase. These are the true Vessels of the Line, which is not the case with the first 4 phases that emerged by the power of Binding (Intercourse) by Striking from the Curtain upwards to the Root, as explained above—these are considered merely Roots of the Vessels, since the Power of the Curtain is not able to ascend with the Returning Light upwards, and so the phase one finds here is Light alone, without any impurity of the Curtain—and so these are not true Vessels, but the Root of Vessels. But afterwards, when the Returning Light spreads downwards from the Curtain, it leads with it the impurity of the Curtain as well, thereby becoming a phase of true Vessels. (This is not the place for too lengthy an explanation).

CHAPTER 3

ESSENCE AND MATERIAL OF THE VESSELS

Explaining: The essence and material of the Vessels in 2 topics:

1. Three fundamental aspects of the Vessels:
   a) Their material essence;
   b) Their power of Restriction;
   c) Their Curtain.

2. The material essence in the Vessels has 2 phases:
   a) The Kingdom of the Upper which was the first material in the Lower;
   b) The Light drawn into the latter material is distinguished as the phase of the Lower itself.

23) Now we may begin to understand the question raised above about the order of the Sefirot of Straightness, where the more impure Sefira is higher and more important, which goes against reason, since reason would suggest that every purer Vessel clothes a higher, more important Light, and every impurer Vessel clothes a lower less important Light (See above). From what has been said you will understand this, but we must explain further the 4 phases of the Desire which are the Vessels of the Sefirot called: Wisdom, Intelligence, the Small Face, and Kingdom, and their root, called Crown (The Small

Face alone contains 6 Sefirot: HG"T NH"Y), all of which require a lengthy explanation.

24) These Vessels have 3 fundamental aspects: The first is the essential material of the Vessel. The 2nd is the Power of the Restriction in the Vessel, which means removal from the great Desire to Receive, of its own choice and free will, not because of the power of the Upper over it. The 3rd is the phase of the Curtain in it, which means removal from the great Desire to Receive by the controlling power of the Upper over it, which is to say removal by force, not by choice. We shall explain each of the three separately.

25) We already know that the material of the Vessel is composed of 4 levels, one below the other, of the Desire to Receive, the higher being the reason and cause for the emergence of the level below it: thus, the Root causes the revelation of Desire in phase 1, Phase 1 causes the revelation of the Desire of phase 2, Phase 2 causes the revelation of the Desire in phase 3, Phase 3 causes the revelation of the Desire in phase 4. This devolvement, according to the necessary relationship of cause and effect has already been well explained above, volume 1, (*Inner Light*, chapter 1, N, begin.: "The reason," see above, since I hesitate to repeat that lengthy explanation, but the reader is urged to refer to it since the following explanations depend upon it).

26) Indeed, to be precise, each of these 4 phases has 2 distinct aspects: the first is the amount of material which reached it from its cause. The second is the amount of material in its essence which is affected by the Light which clothes itself in

it. We know that the Desire found in a level is called the Kingdom of that level. Even where no Vessel is recognizable, which is to say in the Endless, PB''G, we also term the Desire found there as Kingdom of the Endless, PB''G, as indicated by the secret meaning of the words: "He and His Name are One." "Name" is a term for the Sefira of Kingdom, and "and His Name" is the numerical equivalent of "Desire."

27) Now we will explain the two aspects in each of the 4 phases. The Root of the Level, on which the Light of the Endless resides, is called the Crown of that level. We know that the Upper Light has not only the Desire to Influence and Improve all of existence in the Worlds it created—however it does not have, Heaven forbid, any of "The Desire to Receive." This has been well explained, at length, in the *Inner Reflection*, volume 1, to which the reader should refer. The Kingdom of Crown is the cause for phase 1, since whatever is Desire in the Upper becomes necessity and compulsion in the Lower (Sefira). Thus the Desire to Benefit and Influence, which is Kingdom of Crown, becomes a phase of the "Desire to Receive" in phase 1, called Wisdom. We find then that the Kingdom of Crown itself, descended, was clothed, and became the Desire to Receive of phase 1, which is to say its actual material: because the Desire in phase 1 is the material in that phase, and the Upper Light called "Living" is clothed in this material. Thus we find that Kingdom of Crown became the material of the Sefira called Wisdom. This is the first aspect we have to distinguish in the material of phase 1.

28) The 2nd aspect is: after the Upper Light has spread (called Living) into the Kingdom of Crown, (which is the

material of Wisdom) at which time the Kingdom of Crown received its aspect of true material of phase 1, which is to say Kingdom of Crown, the Desire to Influence included in the Upper Light becomes a phase of the Desire to Receive, and the first material of phase 1, as explained. However this sufficed only for the root of phase 1, in other words, so that this Desire to Receive will draw the Upper Light into itself, which we may term (like the first material of the Sefira of Wisdom) as still being in the form of an Emanator and Crown. When does it cease to be Emanator and Crown, becoming Emanation and Wisdom, called phase 1? Only when the Desire to Receive drew into itself the "Living" Light related to it, then it ceased to be an Emanator, and is henceforth called Emanation or Wisdom—understand this well. Thus 2 distinctions in the material of the Vessel called Wisdom have been explained: the first is called the Upper Kingdom—before it has drawn its proper Light; the second is called the Vessel of Wisdom itself which is Kingdom of Wisdom, since the Vessel is always called Kingdom.

29) Thus we may understand the material of phase 2, called Intelligence, whose cause is the Desire included in phase 1, called Wisdom, which is to say only Kingdom of Wisdom, because the Desire at a Level is always called a Vessel or the Kingdom of that level, as explained above. This Kingdom of Wisdom was clothed and became the first material in the Sefira of Intelligence in order to draw the Light proper to it. This is the first aspect in the material of phase 2, called Intelligence. Afterwards, when it has drawn the Light proper to it, called Soul, then its material emerged from the phase of Kingdom

of Wisdom (which is phase 1) and received its own form, which is phase 2, called Intelligence.

30) In this way we may understand the material of phase 3 called the Small Face, which Kingdom of Intelligence causes, becoming the first material of the Small Face, which is phase 3, which is to say that it will draw the Light proper to the Small Face, called Spirit. The second aspect is: after it has drawn and received its Light, when its material emerges from Kingdom of Intelligence becoming Kingdom of the Small Face, as explained above.

31) The two aspects of the material of the 4th phase are similar. The Kingdom of the Small Face was its cause, being clothed and becoming the first material of the 4th phase, called Kingdom, until it had received sufficient Light of Life, proper to it, at which time the Kingdom of the Small Face emerged from the Small Face, becoming the 4th phase, which is Kingdom of Kingdom.

32) However, understand that although we have explained and determined an aspect of Receival for every individual phase, this refers only to the drawing of the Light, since every phase draws the Straight Light proper to it, but only the 4th phase is a true Vessel, worthy of the name Vessel of Receival to the Emanation—this is not true of the 3 preceding phases, as explained above.

CHAPTER 4

FOUR ASPECTS OF IMPURITY

Explaining: An exact explanation of the 4 aspects of impurity in the fourfold manner of the Rabbis. (Pesahim, 25)

Aspect 1: Not Possible and Not Intending.

Aspect 2: Possible and Not Intending.

Aspect 3: Not Possible and Intending.

Aspect 4: Possible and Intending.

33) In order to provide a full and exact explanation I shall explain by citing the teachings of Our Rabbis, (May their Memory be Blessed) See Pesahim, 25b: "It was stated: [As to forbidden] benefit that comes to a man against his will, Abaye said: It is permitted; while Ravah maintained: It is forbidden, Where it is possible [to avoid it], yet he intends [to benefit], none dispute that it is forbidden. If it is impossible [to avoid it], and he does not intend [to benefit], none dispute that it is permitted. They differ where it is possible [to avoid it] and he does not intend [to benefit]." "Possible" means "possible to avoid" and "Intending" means "intending to benefit," as in the case of a forbidden aroma (*op. cit.*).

34) We find in their words 4 modes of receiving pleasure: the first is "Not possible" for him to separate himself from it

"and not intending" to approach and take pleasure, in which case everyone agrees that receiving of forbidden pleasure is not punishable, since we do not consider as willing receival a case in which one has no intention to receive the forbidden pleasure, nor any longing to approach it, so as to enjoy it.

35) The second mode is the case where it is "Possible" for him to separate himself and "He does not Intend" to appraoch and take pleasure. As for Receiving forbidden pleasure in this manner: Abayeh and Ravah disagree. Abayeh said: even though it is "Possible" which is to say he has the idea to remove himself from it and not take pleasure in the forbidden, nevertheless he is permitted to approach and take pleasure from it, because "He does not intend," in other words: there is no longing in his heart to approach the forbidden; thus it is not considered receival even though he approaches and takes pleasure in the forbidden. Ravah says: since it is "Possible" for him not to approach and derive pleasure from the forbidden, thus it is forbidden for him to approach and derive pleasure from it, even though he does not long to approach the forbidden and take pleasure in it.

36) The third mode is "Not Possible and Intending," which is to say, it is "Not Possible" for him to separate and remove himself from the forbidden pleasure, so as not to enjoy it; "Intending," meaning that he longs to take pleasure in the forbidden. As for receiving forbidden pleasure in this manner, everyone agrees that it is forbidden, because even though is it not possible for him, and he has no choice to remove himself from the forbidden pleasure, still and all, because there is longing in his heart to approach and take forbidden pleasure, this

longing is considered receival of forbidden pleasure and he has committed a sin—there are those who say that even in this case Abayeh thought no sin was committed (See Pesahim, 25b).

37) The 4th mode is "Possible and With Intent" which is to say: It is "Possible" for him to remove himself from the forbidden pleasure, and "with Intent," i.e. he longs to approach and take forbidden pleasure. In this case all agree that it is forbidden, since this is the worst case of taking forbidden pleasure, since he longs to take forbidden pleasure, and yet is able to abstain but he does not. Thus it represents the most extreme form of the Desire to Receive, which everyone agrees is forbidden—even those who asserted that Abayeh permits the 3rd mode of Receiving pleasure admit that it is forbidden in this case (see the Gemarah, Pesahim 25b).

38) Now we have found in the words of the Rabbis quoted above, the exact way to define each of the 4 aspects of "The Desire to Receive," to distinguish between sinful and permitted receival of pleasure—they have provided us with 4 levels, one beneath the other, of forbidden pleasure taking, dependent on the "Desire to Receive" in the sinner. In 3 cases: Not Possible, without Intent; Possible, without Intent; Not Possible, with Intent, not everyone agrees that the pleasure is forbidden—only in the 4th case do all agree that pleasure is forbidden, as explained above.

39) We see that our Wise men, May their Memory be blessed, have combined 2 things: the "Possibility" of avoiding the forbidden pleasure and the matter of "Longing" or attraction to the forbidden pleasure—from the combination of

these 2 things there arise 4 possible cases. Now we shall apply the foregoing discussion of our study of the Upper Worlds, which are the roots for all types of Desire to be found in existence, and from the lower world we can learn about the Upper World.

40) In phase 1, called Wisdom and also Living, there are 2 aspects (as explained above, *Inner Reflection*, volume 2, 27). The first is its first material; we already know (N.B. above, *Inner Reflection*, volume 2, 23, begin.: "Now we may begin") that it is its phase of Kingdom of the Upper, which is to say Kingdom of the Crown which received the form of the Desire to Receive, so that with the renewal of this form Kingdom of Crown received a new name, phase 1. We already know that when Spiritual Substance receives a new form it achieves a power in its own right, so with the Kingdom of Crown, which is the Desire to Influence in the Emanator, when its Desire to Emanate is born, then, to be sure, it does not require a creating Vessel, Heaven forbid, rather its Desire works at once, which is to say, receiving the form of "the Desire to Receive," which is the first material of the Emanation, as explained above—this is what is called phase 1.

41) Remember that Spiritual Substance can not disappear, and when we say that Kingdom of Crown received the form of phase 1, this does not mean that Kingdom of Crown, Heaven forbid, disappeared from or was removed from the Crown, but rather that the Kingdom of Crown remained at its first height without change—compare the lighting of a candle with another candle, the first candle losing nothing—so the Kingdom of Crown which received phase 1 lost, in so doing,

nothing of the Crown, instead it added a new phase; in other words, Kingdom of Crown stayed in its place, complete and at its former height, but another phase of Kingdom of Crown was added to it, which is to say, the phase of Kingdom which received phase 1, becoming the first material in the Sefira of Wisdom—keep this in mind when reading what follows and you will not be confused.

42) The second aspect is the material of that Vessel after it has received its Light, for then the Vessel is completed and is called "Wisdom," in other words, before it received its Light it is called by the name of its phase alone, which is phase 1, and it is not yet the phase of the Vessel of Wisdom, but rather Kingdom of Crown. One may compare the fetus in the mother's womb which is not named until it sees the Light. So with the first material before it receives its Light— it is not called Wisdom, but is still considered part of Kingdom of Crown; but afterwards, when the material draws its Light, called "Living", then the Vessel obtains its distinctive name, which is "Wisdom." (N.B. above, 27, begin.: "Now we will explain..."). These two aspects must be understood for each Sefira. They are: the Vessel before receiving its Light, still called by its Upper name, and the Vessel after receiving its Light, thereafter considered in its own regard.

43) Now one may understand that phase 1 which is Wisdom is distinguished as "Not Possible and without Intent" since, with respect to its first material which is Kingdom of Crown, which received renewal of form of phase 1 when the Sefira of Wisdom had not yet arisen in its own respect, as explained above, therefore, the revelation of this Desire to

Receive is, to be sure, distinguished as "Not Possible," with respect to the Sefira of Wisdom itself. It is also considered "Not Possible" with respect to the Kingdom of Crown since it is impossible for Kingdom of Crown to emanate Wisdom without Wisdom already having "the Desire to Receive," since receival of Abundance without the Desire to Receive is a great burden and compulsion against the nature of the Emanator which tends to improve and give pleasure, as is well known. It is also distinguished as "Without Intent" which means that there is no drawing and longing to receive Light. We already know that there is no completeness of the Desire before the revelation of longing and drawing to the Light (N.B., as explained above, volume 1, chapter 1, N, begin.: "Now you can understand..."). It is also thoroughly explained above that longing is not revealed except when the Light and Abundance are not in the Vessel, since then only is it apt that the Vessel long for Light—but this can't be revealed when the Vessel is still full of its Light (N.B. see above). Therefore, since the aforementioned Vessel of Wisdom is full of its own Light it has not yet the longing for the Abundance, and so Wisdom is considered "without Intent," which means that it does not draw and long for the Abundance, as explained.

44) Phase 2, which is Intelligence is defined as: "Possible and without Intent," because with respect to its first material (N.B. as explained above *Inner Reflection*, volume 2, 29 begin.: "Thus we may understand...") which is its Kingdom of the Upper, which is Kingdom of Wisdom, which received the renewal of form of phase 2 by means of its overcoming action; (N.B. as thoroughly explained above, volume 1, part 1, N,

begin.: "And the reason for the…"). It is indeed this over-coming action of the Desire that is distinguished as "Pos-sible," in other words, it was possible for it not to awaken this overcoming action of the Desire. It is further distinguished as "without Intent" because it is Kingdom of Wisdom, and is full of its Light, and therefore longing is not revealed in it, as explained above—understand that any increment in the revelation of the Desire in phase 2 over phase 1 is only an aspect of the "Possible," which is to say the overcoming action of the Desire in phase 2 which comes from the power of the Emanation itself. (N.B. above, volume 1, part 1, N, begin.: "Now…").

45) One may not ask: Was it not also "Possible" for King-dom of Crown which became phase 1 in the Sefira of Wisdom not to receive the phase of renewal of the Desire to Receive? Why was phase 1 distinguished as "Not Possible?" Indeed, there is a great distinction to be made here, because the King-dom of Crown did not have the possibility of emanating the Emanation without it having "the Desire to Receive," as explained above, whereas Kingdom of Wisdom, which is an actual phase of the Emanation was absolutely able to make due with its own phase of the Desire to Receive without awakening the Desire to Influence (which is phase 2) and drawing the Light of Mercy since the Light of Living is ab-solutely sufficient for the Emanation, with no need of any addition.

46) Phase 3, which is the Small Face, is distinguished as "not Possible and with Intent." It is "Not Possible" because after the second phase was awakened and drew the Light of

Mercy the Light of Wisdom in the Emanation was hindered because the Desire to Influence is contrary to phase 1 which is the Desire to Receive, which is where the Light of Wisdom is found. And since the Light of Wisdom is the fundamental life of the Countenance on which account this Light is termed "Living" (as explained above), therefore Kingdom of Intelligence returned and drew the illumination of the Light of Wisdom into its Light of Mercy, and when Kingdom of Intelligence drew and caused this renewal of form it emerged from phase 2, becoming phase 3 (N.B. as explained above, *Inner Reflection*, volume 2, 30, begin.: "In this way...") which is called the Small Face.

47) This drawing which is phase 3 has 2 aspects we must distinguish: the first is "Not Possible," which is to say, that it has no other choice on account of the Living Light which was lacking in the Emanation. The second is "with Intent" because in this case there is longing for the illumination of Wisdom which it drew, because it drew it when it was empty, for phase 2 was a covering on the Light of Wisdom (as explained above), and it contained only the Light of Mercy, without Wisdom. Therefore its Kingdom which drew the illumination of Wisdom, this drawing is the phase of longing, being called therefore "With Intent," as explained above. Thus the phase of the Small Face is called "Not Possible and with Intent," as explained.

48) The 4th phase, Kingdom, is described as "Possible and with Intent": Possible because there already exists illumination of Wisdom in the Small Face, which is to say, in the phase 3 (as explained above), and Kingdom of the Small Face

is not forced to repeat this overcoming action so as to draw the Light of Wisdom in a greater quantity than is to be found in phase 3; "With Intent", because this overcoming action after the Light of Wisdom was in the phase of longing, which is to say at a time when it did not possess the Light of Wisdom, at which time the longing is revealed, as explained above.

49) One may not ask: Doesn't phase 3 have the illumination of Wisdom (as explained above) as a result of which the 4th phase is called "Possible", and so how is the longing for the Light of Wisdom revealed in the 4th phase? Indeed one must understand quite clearly that there is a vast difference between the illumination of Wisdom and the Light of Wisdom. The illumination of Wisdom refers to the fact that the essence of the level is the Light of Mercy which, however, receives illumination from the Light of Wisdom—but this is not the case with the Light of Wisdom, the essence of whose Light is entirely Wisdom, and not Mercy, in any way. As for the life of the level, the amount of the illumination of Wisdom (in the 3rd phase, which is the Small Face) suffices, and so the Kingdom of the Small Face which overcame with its Desire to draw the Light of Wisdom was not forced to do so, rather there was longing in it after the essence of the Light of Wisdom which is far superior to the illumination of Wisdom in phase 3. With respect to the aforementioned Light of Wisdom, it is found to be empty and so it stands to reason that longing should arise, as explained.

50) It has been explained that not all of the Desires are considered Vessels of receival, only the 4th phase alone, since Desire is not considered a phase of receival unless the 2 con-

ditions of "Possible" and "With Intent" are met. Which means: that receival is not forced, and that "Longing" arises. As for phase 3, even though it has longing to receive, which is to say "With Intent," nevertheless since it is forced to receive (this being essential to its nature, as explained above), it is not considered a Vessel of Receival. As for phase 2, even though it is not forced to receive, nevertheless since there is no longing, it is not considered a Vessel of Receival—we need not even mention phase 1, which has neither one nor the other, since it must receive its Light, which is its essence, and it has no longing, and so it surely is a completely weak Desire.

CHAPTER 5

RESTRICTION AND THE CURTAIN

Explaining: Restriction and the Curtain in 4 topics:

1. The Contraction was equal on all sides.

2. The Curtain; since all continuation of Light is in the 4th phase there must be a preventing Power which keeps the Light from spreading to the 4th phase—the Power is called the Curtain.

3. Two aspects to Kingdom:
   a) Contracted so as not to receive Light of its own Desire. This occurs in Circles;
   b) Contracted because of the Preventive Power of the Curtain. This occurs in Sefirot of Straightness.

4. The Upper Light is at perfect rest, never ceasing to illumine for even an instant. When the Emanation longs for it, the Upper Light supplies it with Light.

51) Now that we understand well the 4 levels of the Desire to receive, one below the other, we will explain contraction and the Curtain and the difference between them. Contraction has already been thoroughly explained in volume 1, and in the *Inner Light* above—there is no need to repeat the entire explanation. The essential matter for our discussion is the

likeness of the Contraction (N.B. above *Inner Light*, volume 1, part 1, R, begin.: "Circle etc...").

52) It is explained above that because the Light of the End-less is totally equal it was necessary that it contract itself equally in every respect; in other words, so that all 4 of the phases which were contracted are at the same height, without any distinctions of purity or impurity, which normally account for the 4 levels one below the other, up to the 4th level which is impurer and lower than all the others—but in this case they are equal. What the Contraction has added to the original state of the Endless, PB"G, is merely the 4 phases as they are caused by and devolved from one another, in a cause and effect relationship: phase 1 induces and causes the revelation of phase 2, phase 2 causes phase 3, and phase 3 causes phase 4—but they are equal in purity and height as explained above.

53) As for this cause and effect relationship which separates them into 4 phases, it was not revealed in the Endless, PB"G before the Contraction, since in the Endless even the inclusive aspect of the Vessel is not recognizable, rather it is entirely made up of Light (as is explained in volume 1), but after the Light of the Endless has withdrawn from those four phases they became recognizable and the following was revealed: as for the Light itself, what they contained before the Con-traction and the 4 phases themselves—they remained void of Light since after the Contraction it was revealed that these 4 phases are not one with the Light of the Endless, PB"G, as they indeed seemed to be before the Contraction. Compare a candle inside a torch which is not recognized until it has been separated from the torch—understand this well.

54) An apparent difficulty is that since the main effect of the Contraction was on phase 4 it would seem that this phase is not worthy to receive Light, however, the first 3 phases, which the Contraction did not effect, should receive Light, thus it follows that phase 4 is lower than the first three phases.

55) The answer is, however, that the Contraction of the Light from phase 4 was not on account of its inferiority, Heaven forbid, since we are still dealing with Kingdom of the Endless, PB''G, where the fourth phase was the Light of the Endless, PB''G, itself, and how can one even suspect that the Contraction was on account of the inferiority of the 4th phase? Instead, the Contraction took place merely on account of the Kingdom's desire to ornament as brilliantly as possible and adhere entirely to the Emanator, a matter of as great an equality of form to the Emanator as possible (N.B. above volume 1, part 1, R, begin.: "The Contraction...") and so the height of the fourth phase was not lowered even after the Contraction.

56) Now we shall explain the matter of the Curtain made on the fourth phase which is Kingdom; for when the World of the Contraction, which is Kingdom of the Endless, PB''G (clothed, as we know, in all levels beginning from Kingdom of the Upper which becomes its first material [see above, 27]), indeed, when this contracted Kingdom drew the Upper Light towards 3 phases alone, behold, this drawing was forced by the longing in its 4th phase, for the first 3 phases are in no way Vessels of Receival or drawing. Thus it was necessary that the Upper Light be drawn to all 4 phases, even to the fourth phase, but in order for the Light not to reach the fourth

phase it was required of the fourth phase to acquire one additional power to prevent the Light from extending to it.

57) This new power which was added is called "Curtain," and it is the root cause of the extension of the Light of the Line to the three phases: for the Contraction which it effected which removed the Desire to Receive from the fourth phase suffices only to remove the Upper Light from it alone, however, afterwards it drew the Light forcing the awakening of its fourth phase in order to continue the new extension, and so if there were no new power to extend the Light, the Light would once again reach the fourth phase, since the main cause of the extension of the Light of the Line to the 3 phases is only the "Curtain" which was made fresh opposite the Light. Understand well these two phases: Restriction or Contraction and the Curtain, for they are vital to an understanding of what follows.

58) Understand the difference between the Contraction of Kingdom of the Endless, which is removed from the great Desire to Receive out of a chosen desire for greater equality of form with the Emanator, and between the Curtain, which is the power of prevention, with control and force, not allowing the Light to reach the fourth phase.

59) The reason for this is that even though the Contraction and the Curtain were both made by the Kingdom of the Endless, PB"G, as explained above, nevertheless we already know that when Spiritual Substance acquires a new form in addition to its original form it is distinguished as 2 Spiritual Substances and 2 phases, as far from one another as the extent in change

of form between the 2 forms; for just as material things can be split with an axe, and are divided by distance and extent, so Spiritual Substances are divided from one another by renewal of form, and are removed either more or less from one another according to the extent in change of form between the 2 forms.

60) Therefore, after the above mentioned Kingdom has continued the Light of the Line to the 3 phases this continuation enters a new phase (in addition to the form of the Contraction), in such a way that this Kingdom now has 2 phases: the first is the Contracted Kingdom which is the first phase made in Kingdom of the Endless, PB"G, receiving the new form called "Contracted Kingdom." Afterwards when this Kingdom has continued after the Light of the 3 phases, a new form was born and emerged called "Curtain," opposite the Light, preventing it from appearing in phase 4. We know, to be sure, that every Desire in the Upper World has control over any branch which comes out of it, and since the Curtain is a branch of the Contracted Kingdom, therefore, even though the Kingdom contracted itself of its own will, without control by anything higher up than itself, still and all the Curtain which is born from it is entirely controlled by the contraction since it is a second level in the World of Contraction, as explained above.

61) It follows from what has been said above that there are two phases of Kingdom: the first is "Contracted Kingdom" and the second is Kingdom with a Curtain. Note that this is all that sets apart Sefirot of Circles and Sefirot of Straightness, called Line. Of the Ten Sefirot of Circles, one finds their

Kingdom is Contracted Kingdom, without a Curtain, as explained above, and of the Ten Sefirot of Straightness we find that their Kingdom is modified by the Curtain described above and further explained below.

62) Now one may well understand the matter of the Returning Light which ascends by means of "Binding by Striking" from the meeting of the Upper Light with the Curtain on the fourth phase which we started to explain above (18, begin.: "The answer is..."). Understand that the reason for what we stated above (that the Upper Light does not enforce the Contraction of the Emanation, but descends to spread out in the fourth phase, N.B. above) is because the Emanation itself draws the Light inevitably from the outset, for it has already been explained (above volume 1, part 2, *Inner Light*, B) that the Upper Light is always at absolute rest, never ceasing to illumine things below it for a moment, because it does not fall subject to, Heaven forbid, chance or change; and every mention of the spreading of the Upper Light refers to the drawing of the Upper Light by the Emanation according to the latter's desire to receive, which is to say its longing as explained above (*Inner Reflection*, volume 2, 50, begin.: "It has been explained...").

63) At the same moment that the Emanation longs to receive from the Upper Light it immediately draws the Upper Light to itself. Compare the lighting of one candle by another, where the first candle loses nothing, so, at the moment when the Emanation draws to itself the Upper Light, the Upper Light loses nothing on account of the small quantity of Light drawn by the Emanation and so it is not activated or extended

on account of its being drawn by the Emanation, rather we merely term the continuation of the Emanation as the spreading of the Upper Light—remember this in what follows, since we speak always of the spreading of the Upper Light, when we refer to the continuation of the Emanation itself by means of its longing alone.

64) Therefore, after the Contraction (when the Kingdom of the Endless, PB''G, drew the Upper Light, since it drew it by means of the longing in its fourth phase, as explained above) the Upper Light is drawn to the fourth phase as well, however, by the power of Curtain to prevent the Light from spreading to the fourth phase, this portion of Light returned backwards to fulfill its initial impulse to have the Light reach only 3 phases. However that portion of the Light that the Curtain returned to its Root (which is the portion bound for phase 4), did not disappear from it, but became a great Light clothing the 3 phases of the Upper Light from the place of the Curtain upwards to the Root, so that this Returning Light becomes a vessel of receival for the 3 phases of the Upper Light instead of the fourth phase as explained above (*Inner Reflection*, 21, begin.: ''Now we can understand...'').

CHAPTER 6

THE CURTAIN AND THE
RETURNING LIGHT

Explaining: The reason why the Curtain of the fourth phase sends up Returning Light to the Crown, the third phase to Wisdom, etc.—because the extent of Returning Light depends upon how much Light would have been clothed in the fourth phase, were it not for the Curtain which deflects the Light. Also explaining that the Ten Sefirot of Straight Light are from above to below, the purer being higher, and that the Ten Sefirot of Returning Light are from below to above, the impurer being higher.

65) From what has been explained one can understand throughly the size and extent of this Returning Light which is neither greater nor smaller than the extent of the Light which the Curtain deflected, that is to say the portion which would otherwise have spread in the fourth phase had not the Curtain returned it. It ascended and clothed the phases of the Upper Light as follows: third phase called the Small Face, the second phase called Intelligence, and phase 1 called Wisdom, as well as the Root, called Crown; this is why phase 4 itself divided into the same 4 levels which its Returning Light clothed, and these 4 levels were ordered one on top of the other in the Vessel of phase 4 itself, because the Light appropriate to it went up and clothed these 4 levels. This is why

the fourth phase is considered a Root phase, called the Crown of this Returning Light.

66) Now we shall discover the 2 phases of the 10 Sefirot in the Emanation which are: 10 Sefirot from above to below and 10 Sefirot from below to above, for there are 10 Sefirot in the Upper Light: the Root, called Crown of the Upper Light, and 4 phases drawn from the Crown, the first called Wisdom, the second called Intelligence, the third called the Small Face (including 6 Sefirot: HG"T, NH"Y), and the fourth called Kingdom—their order being from above to below, which means from the pure to the impure, in other words every purer Sefira is more important, and the purest of all, which is the Root, is called Crown. Next, slightly less pure than Crown, is Wisdom, and so on, until we reach the impurest of all, which is Kingdom, the least important of all.

67) There is a second set of Sefirot in the Emanation which are approximately reversed compared to the 10 Sefirot of the Upper Light described above. They are the 10 Sefirot in the Returning Light which ascends from the Curtain in the fourth phase, as explained above, and they clothe the 10 Sefirot of the Upper Light. Their order is from below to above, which means from the impure to the pure, with the impure being first in order, every purer Sefira being lower, which is opposite from the order of the 10 Sefirot of the Upper Light.

68) The impurest of all, which is the fourth phase, is most important of all, since it is the Root of all 10 Sefirot of the Returning Light, since the entire Returning Light is really nothing more than a portion of the Light belonging to the

fourth phase which the Curtain turned away. Thus the fourth phase is distinguished as a phase of Crown, which means a Root phase, as is well known.

69) The third phase, which is not as impure as the fourth, is distinguished as the Sefira of Wisdom of the Returning Light, which is to say it is second in order to the Crown. The second phase, purer than phase 3, is third in order from the Crown, which is to say it is Intelligence. The first phase, purer than phase 2, is fourth in order of height from the Crown, which means it is the Sefira of the Small Face, which includes 6 Sefirot: HG"T, NH"Y. The Crown of Straight Light, purer than any of these Sefirot is considered with respect to the Returning Light merely as a phase of Kingdom; in other words lower in height than all the others, because the impurer is the more important, and the purer is the less important, because the levels extend from the impure to the pure—N.B.

70) The fourth phase itself, by virtue of the power of its Returning Light which spreads to all 10 Sefirot, divides into 10 Sefirot, that is to say 4 phases and Crown, because the fourth phase itself is the Crown of the Returning Light (which is to say, its Root as explained above), and the 9 Sefirot of the Returning Light which spread and ascend from it are its branches, which to be sure, are included and continue to exist in their Root—therefore phase 4 itself is distinguished as having 5 phases: Crown and the 4 usual phases, ordered from below to above.

71) This will further clarify the assertion made earlier (*Inner Reflection*, volume 2, 8, begin.: "However, with Sefirot...")

that the size of the Returning Light is measured by the amount of impurity in the Curtain, since the impurer Curtain (which is the Curtain of phase 4) reaches to the Crown with the Returning Light it deflects. The Curtain of phase 3 reaches only to Wisdom, the Curtain of phase 2 only to Intelligence, and the Curtain of phase 1 only to the Small Face. As for a Curtain without even the impurity of phase 1, resembling the Root, it sends back no Light whatsoever, but merely the phase of Kingdom alone (N.B. above). From what has been explained one can understand the matter of the purification of the Curtain in the 5 phases mentioned above. It is a matter of the division of phase 4 itself into the 5 phases mentioned here so that the Curtain may ascend and be purified from level of impurity to level of impurity, all found in the fourth phase—the reason is explained below.

CHAPTER 7

PURIFICATION AND EMERGENCE
OF THE FIVE LEVELS

Explaining: The matter of the purification of the Curtain and an explanation of the emergence of the 5 levels: KH''B, Z''A and Kingdom, one below the other, on account of the purification of the Curtain.

72) To understand the purification of the Curtain one must first understand two things. The first is that the power of prevention in the Curtain is equally balanced with the impurity which is the longing in the fourth phase, as are the two arms of a scale. The reason for this is simple, for if the longing to receive is great, then it requires great power to prevent itself from receiving and if the longing is small there is no great need to prevent itself from receiving; thus the power of prevention in the Curtain is balanced by the amount of impurity in the fourth phase, either more or less.

73) The second thing one must understand is that the nature of the surrounding Light which is not clothed in the Emanation is to purify the impurity in the fourth phase, slowly, according to the order of the 4 phases, until it completely purifies all of the impurity, first purifying from phase 4 to phase 3, afterwards to phase 2, and then to phase 1, after which it is completely purified, with no impurity remaining whatsoever.

74) The reason for this is that the Surrounding Light refers to that Upper Light which can not be clothed in the Emanation on account of the Curtain which prevents it from spreading beyond its height, so that it remains outside of the Countenance and surrounds it, which is to say illumines it at a distance. Because the Surrounding Light wishes to illumine the interior of the Countenance as well, as was its habit in the Endless where it illumined the fourth phase as well, therefore it strikes the Curtain and purifies it, which is to say, it nullifies the impurity and hardness in it so that it can be clothed.

75) At first the Curtain prevails and pushes it back, and then the Light prevails and purifies the Curtain. But it nullifies only that phase of impurity upon which "Binding by Striking" occurred. If the "Binding by Striking" occurred in the fourth phase then it nullifies the impurity of the fourth phase which prevents it from being clothed in the Countenance, leaving alone the impurity of the third phase, since it has nothing to do with it. If the "Binding by Striking" took place in the impurity of the third phase then it nullifies only the impurity of the third phase leaving the impurity of the second phase, and so, in like manner (as explained in *Ten Luminous Emanations*, volume 4, *Inner Light*, part 1).

76) We already know that any change in form in Spiritual Substance means that the first form does not disappear (since Spiritual Substance cannot disappear), instead there occurs an addition of form. Thus one may understand that the fourth phase which was purified to its third phase is distinguished as emerging from this Emanation to a new Emanation added

on to the first whose fourth phase is not the fourth phase of the fourth phase, but the third phase of the fourth phase. However the first Emanation did not undergo any change whatsoever on account of this purification.

77) It was explained above that the Upper Light does not cease to illumine the lower (Emanations) for even a moment; the matter of its extension to the Emanation depends only on the preparedness of its Vessels, which is to say according to the extent of the Desire to Receive in the Emanations, and as long as the Emanations is aroused and longs for the Upper Light it fulfills its end, to the extent of its Desire, as explained above (N.B. *Inner Reflection*, volume 2, 63, begin.: "At the same moment..."). Therefore after the fourth phase has been purified into its third phase and has emerged as a new, distinct Emanation, it drew the Upper Light, and then 10 new Sefirot of the Upper Light emerged in it from above to below, along with 10 new Sefirot of Returning Light, from below to above, just in the same manner as the spreading of the first Emanation. But there is a great distinction between them in the extent of their Light, for the new Emanation is missing the level of Crown, reaching only to Wisdom.

78) The reason that the level of Crown is missing in the second Emanation is because it does not contain the impurity of the fourth phase of the fourth phase which in the Returning Light is the Crown of the fourth phase; therefore the Curtain returned the Upper Light only from Wisdom on down, which is to say, according to the amount of Light which would have come to the third phase of the fourth phase. This is not the case with the Crown of the fourth phase which would not

have spread even if the Curtain had not prevented it, for the Vessel which drew the Upper Light drew only from Wisdom on downwards at first, and so the Curtain did not deflect the Light of the Crown but only the Light of Wisdom downwards, and so the Light of the Crown is missing from this Returning Light. Because there is no Light of the Crown from the Returning Light there is likewise not any Light of the Crown of the Upper Light since there is no Light which can be clothed in the Emanation without the Returning Light to clothe it, since it is its Vessel of Receival (as explained above, *Inner Reflection*, volume 2, 21, begin.: "Now one can understand") thus it reaches only to the height of Wisdom.

79) The rule is that any drawing of Light takes place only in the fourth phase of the Emanation, even if there is no intention of drawing Light there. The reason for this is that the impurity above the fourth phase is not worthy to draw Light (as explained above, *Inner Reflection*, volume 2, chapter 5, 56, begin.: "Now we can explain...") even phase 1 in the fourth phase is more worthy to draw Light than the actual phase 3 (of the straight light) which is higher, that is to say purer than the entire fourth phase. Therefore, if the impurity has left the fourth phase, Light from the Endless, PB"G, would not be drawn. And since the drawing must be by the fourth phase, and moreover the fourth phase must prevent the Light from spreading out within it because of the Contraction in the fourth phase, for these reasons the fourth phase established the Curtain which fulfills the following functions: when the Light spreads out and reaches the fourth phase the Curtain is awakened and returns this portion of Light back to its Root

and the returned portion of Light does not disappear, but instead it becomes the phase of Returning Light, which means that it becomes a phase of a Vessel of Receival for the Upper Light.

80) Thus the fourth phase and the Curtain are one and the same so far as the drawing of Light from the Endless, PB"G, is concerned, for the hardness of the Curtain depends upon the impurity of the fourth phase. Therefore we most often mention the Curtain alone when referring to the drawing of the Light, but we really intend to refer to both, as just explained. Furthermore, for brevity's sake, we speak of the drawing of the Light from the Endless by the Curtain alone, likewise the emergence of the levels one from the other is termed "the purification of the impurity," even though this refers to the hardness of the Curtain. Remember that this refers to the amount of impurity in the fourth phase which causes the 4 phases of hardness in the Curtain.

81) The emergence of the level of Wisdom from the level of Crown was thoroughly explained above: the first 10 Sefirot emerged after the Restriction by means of the meeting of the Upper Light with the Curtain composed of the entire impurity in the fourth phase (as explained above, *Inner Reflection*, volume 2, 64, begin.: "Therefore, after the contraction...") and so it sent up a Returning Light to the full height up to the Root, called Crown, and after this level was complete, from head, middle to foot, part of the impurity of the Curtain was purified from phase 4 to phase 3 (as explained above *Inner Reflection*, volume 2, 74) and since the Curtain had undergone a change in form it emerged from the level of the

Crown to Wisdom, as explained above. Thus, as a result of the meeting of the Light of the Endless with this Curtain which was purified to the third phase, a second set of 10 Sefirot emerged, which reached only to the height of Wisdom, lacking Crown, as explained above (N.B. *Inner Reflection*, volume 2, 78, begin.: "The reason that...").

82) After this level of Kingdom (Wisdom) was completed head, middle to foot the Surrounding Light once again purified a portion of the impurity of the Curtain, which is to say from phase 3 of phase 4 to phase 2 of phase 4, and this new Curtain of phase 2 of phase 4 emerged from the level of Wisdom for the reason cited above with respect to the level of Crown. (See *Inner Reflection*, volume 2, 76, begin.: "We already know..."). From the meeting of the Upper Light with this new Curtain of phase 2, 10 new Sefirot emerged at the level of Intelligence alone, and lacking Crown and Wisdom.

83) The reason that Wisdom is missing from this new level is the same as that mentioned above (N.B. *Inner Reflection*, volume 2, 75, 76) to explain why Crown was missing. Because this fourth phase contains only impurity of phase 2, which is the phase of Intelligence of the fourth phase, its extension was from the outset only from Intelligence downwards; therefore even if the Curtain did not prevent the Upper Light it would not spread to the fourth phase itself, but rather from Intelligence on down. Thus we find that the Curtain did not send back the Crown and Wisdom worthy to the fourth phase, and so Crown and Wisdom are not found in this Returning Light, and since the Returning Light is not there, neither is the Up-

per Light of Crown and Wisdom, since there is no Vessel of Receival for them.

84) After this new level of Intelligence is completed from head to foot, the Surrounding Light once again purified another part of the impurity in the Curtain from phase 2 to phase 1, this also emerging from the level of Intelligence. From the meeting of the Upper Light with the Curtain of phase 1 in the fourth phase 10 new Sefirot emerged at the height of the Small Face. Here the first 3 Sefirot are missing: Crown, Wisdom, Intelligence, for the same reason mentioned above.

85) After the level of the Small Face was completed from head to foot, the last part of the impurity of the fourth phase was purified, and so the entire Curtain was purified, emerging from the level of the Small Face to the level called Kingdom where no new Light was renewed in it, but instead it is illumined by the Small Face, for it is not worthy of being extended (as explained above), therefore it contains only the Light of Life—the remainder of this matter will be explained, with God's help, in volume 3.

CHAPTER 8

DRAWING AND CLOTHING
OF THE VESSELS

Explaining:

1. Why, in the drawing of the Lights, that which is the impurer is greater, and in their being clothed in the Vessels the purer is more important.

2. The reason for the inverse relationship between Vessels and Lights: why with regard to Vessels the Higher are enlarged first, and with regard to Lights the Lower enter first.

3. Why the Circles are distinguished as Light of Life.

86a) It has been thoroughly explained how the extent of influence of the Upper Light on the Emanation depends upon the amount of impurity in the Curtain: greater impurity (as in the fourth phase) effecting the level of Crown, the lesser the level of Wisdom, and so on, until we reach the purest Curtain which is not at all influenced by the Upper Light because it has no impurity, as already explained.

86b) However, all of this refers to the influence over and spreading of the Upper Light to the Emanation, for everything which exercises influence does so over an impure (Emanation), for the more impure the Curtain is the more Upper Light spreads to it (see *Inner Reflection*, volume 2, 62, begin.: "Now one may well..."; the drawing of Light by the fourth phase is called extension of the Upper Light). However, this is not the case with regard to order of receival by the Emanation of the Upper Light. Instead, the more important Light is received in the purer vessel and the less important is received in the impurer Vessel.

87a) This is what was said above (chapter 2, 14, begin.: "One should not...") that anything which influences, influences the impurer (Emanation), but anything which receives, receives in the purer (Emanation)—to explain these matters I shall explain the order of entry of Lights to the Emanation, after the Restoration. Then it receives the Lights bit by bit, according to levels: first it receives Light of Life, afterwards Light of Spirit, and so on until the Individual Light. In the Vessels the order is reversed—first it receives Crown and afterwards Wisdom, and so on.

87b) This is the order: first the Emanation emerges in the form of 10 Vessels: Crown, Wisdom, Intelligence, the Small Face (comprised of HG"T, NH"Y), and Kingdom, in other words the higher Vessels come first. Afterwards when Light of Life influences it, we find that it comes to the Vessel of Crown, which is the purest Vessel. The reason it has no more Light of the Spirit is because the Curtain in the Crown has no more impurity even of phase 1 and the phase Light of the Spirit is influenced only by the meeting of the Upper Light with the Curtain of phase 1. Because the Curtain is in the Vessel of Crown, which means the Curtain is pure, without any impurity at all, therefore it has only Light of Life, which is related to Kingdom.

88) When it obtains the impurity of phase 1, then by means of the meeting of the Upper Light with this Curtain of phase 1, the Light of Spirit is influenced. The place of this Curtain is in the Vessel of Wisdom which is phase 1. However, even though the Curtain of the Vessel of Wisdom drew the Light of the Spirit to the Countenance, nevertheless the Light of the Spirit is clothed in the Vessel of Crown and the Light of Life which was previously in the Crown descends to Wisdom, the reason as explained: that in the order of receival of Lights the most important Light is clothed in the purest Vessel and the less important in the less pure Vessel—this is the reverse of the order of influence, and so Spirit, which is more important than Life ascends and is clothed in the Crown, and Life descends and is clothed in Wisdom.

89) Afterwards, when its Curtain obtains the impurity of phase 2, which means when the Curtain is in the Vessel of Intelligence, then, through the meeting of the Upper Light with this Curtain the Light of the Soul is influenced, a more important Light than the Lights of Spirit or Life. Also, it receives the Light of the Soul in the purest Vessel, the Vessel of Crown, for the Light of Life, which least important of all, is in the Vessel of Wisdom descends to the Vessel of Intelligence where is to be found the Curtain of phase 2, which is now the impurest Vessel of all. The Light Spirit descends from Crown to the Vessel of Wisdom and the Light of the Soul—which is the most important of all—is clothed in the Vessel of the Crown, the purest of all the Vessels.

90) When its Curtain obtains the impurity of phase 3 the Curtain now is in the Vessel of the Small Face, which is phase

3, then, by means of the meeting of the Upper Light with this Curtain of phase 3, the Light of Living is influenced, a Light more important than the Light of the Soul, and so it must be received in the purest Vessel of all. Therefore the Light of Life, the least important of all, descends from the Vessel of Intelligence to the Vessel which is now impurest of all, which is the Vessel of the Small Face, where the Curtain is of phase 3. And this Light of the Spirit which is in Wisdom now descends to Intelligence and the Light of the Soul which is in the Crown now descends to Wisdom. And the Light of Living, most important of all—is clothed in the Vessel of Crown.

91) Afterwards when the Curtain obtains the impurity of the fourth phase, the Curtain is now in the Vessel of Kingdom, which is the fourth phase. Then, by means of the meeting of the Upper Light with this Curtain of the fourth phase the Light of Individual (most important of all) is influenced so that it is received in the purest Vessel of all—the Vessel of Crown. Therefore, the Light of the Life, least important of all, descends from the Small Face to the Vessel of Kingdom which contains the Curtain of the fourth phase, impurest of all. The Light of the Spirit descends from Intelligence to the Vessel of the Small Face; the Light of the Soul descends from Wisdom to the Vessel of Intelligence; and the Light of Living descends from the Crown to the Vessel of Wisdom, and the Light of the Individual which now arrives is clothed in the Crown. And so now every one of the Lights, NRNH''Y,* has reached its appropraite Vessel.

92) Thus one sees the great difference between the order of the influence of the Upper Light on the Countenance, and

the order of the clothing of the Light in the Vessels. For influencing requires the most impure phase of all (for the Light of the Individual does not influence the Countenance unless a Curtain is found in the Vessel of the fourth phase, as explained), for prior to the presence of this impurity, when there was merely a weaker impurity—from phase 3—it was not possible for this important Light called Individual to influence the Countenance; nevertheless, when this important Light is drawn to the Countenance it is not clothed in the Vessel of the fourth phase but in the purest of all, which is in the Vessel of the Crown.

93) In this manner the Living Light, which is influenced only by the Curtain in the Vessel of the Small Face (which is phase 3), nevertheless when it is received by the Emanation, it is not clothed in the Vessel of the Small Face but in the purest Vessel of all, which is the Vessel of the Crown, as explained. In this manner the Light of the Soul is influenced only by the impure Curtain from phase 2 in the Vessel of Intelligence. However, when it is clothed in it, it is then clothed in the Vessel of Crown. Similarly in the Light of the Spirit which is influenced by the Curtain of phase 1 in the Vessel of Wisdom, nevertheless when it is clothed in it, it is not clothed in the Vessel of Wisdom but in the purest Vessel, which is the Vessel of Crown, as explained. Thus each and every Light which comes to the Countenance comes to it first only in the Vessel of the Crown, as was said: any Emanation which receives Light does so in its purest Vessel, even though it was influenced by the impurest Vessel—one must understand this thoroughly.

94) From what has been explained one may also understand why the Circles are not influenced by the Upper Light, but all their Lights must be received from the Light of the Line even though the Vessels of Circles precede the Vessels of Straightness of the Line. The matter is quite simple: the vessels of Circles have no impurity whatsoever, all four of their phases being equal (as explained above, volume 1), part 1, 100 begin.: "Meaning...".). Therefore only the Vessels of Straightness in the Line (which have a Curtain and impurity) are influenced by the Upper Light, and the Circles receive from them.

95) Thus the Light of the Circles is called Light of Life, for the rule is: any level which is not influenced by the Upper Light but receives its illumination from another level—this Light is called Light of Life or Female Light. Because the Circles are not influenced by the Upper Light but receive illumination from the Line, their Light is Female, or Light of Life. As for the Vessels of Straightness, it was explained above (*Inner Reflection*, volume 2, 85, begin.: "After the level...") that if all of the impurity of the Curtain has been purified, then there is no longer influence from the Upper Light, and there is only illumination from the preceding level, called for this reason, Light of Life (N.B. above).

CHAPTER 9

PRIMARY, SECONDARY AND TERTIARY SEFIROT

Explaining: Why each and every primary sefira is composed of ten secondary sefirot, and each of these ten secondary sefirot is composed of ten tertiary sefirot, and so on, without number, *ad infinitum*.

The division of the sefirot into secondary, tertiary, and quaternary sefirot, *ad infinitum*:

96) It is a wondrous law in the Upper Worlds that each and every sefira has ten sefirot of its own, and each of these ten sefirot has ten particular sefirot of its own; furthermore, if one examines one of these particular sefirot one finds that it too has ten particular sefirot of its own, and so on, *ad infinitum*.

97) The reason for this is to be understood in Light of the principle that there is no disappearance of Spiritual Substance (see *Inner Light*, volume 2, part 1, D[1]). It has been explained that it is impossible for any phase of Light to be found in a lower Emanation without the same phase of Light being found in all the Emanations above it, up to the Endless, Praised Be God. Even a very slight illumination which emerges at the lowest level in the Worlds must emerge from the Endless, PB''G, and pass through all the Worlds and levels which precede that lower level at which it finally arrives. Furthermore,

it is impossible that this illumination, when devolving and passing from level to level, should disappear from the first level because it raches the second, and disappear from the second when it reaches the third, and so on, until it reaches the last level which receives it, as would happen to a material object passing from place to place—but this is not the case with Spiritual Substance which is not subject to disappearance or change; instead, every illumination which occupies a level (even if only while passing through it) obtains a permanent place in that level.

98) As for the passage from level to level, there is no diminution whatsoever in the Light, its intensity being the same at each level; compare the lighting of one candle with another candle, in which case the first candle is not at all diminished. So here: when the Light goes from the first level to the second it is found to be complete in both places. In like manner, when the Light goes to the third level it does not disappear from the second, but instead it is found in perfect fulness at both the second and third levels, and so on, as the Light passes through all the levels preceding that last level which is its true recipient (i.e. that level for which the Light left the Endless, PB''G) it is fixed at all the levels it traverses. All this occurs because there is no disappearance of Spiritual Substance, and every Light which has once illumined a Spiritual Substance will never in the slightest way leave that substance, to eternity.

99) From what has been explained, one may well understand the inclusion of ten sefirot, one inside the other, *ad infinitum*. Take, for example, the emergence of the first two sefirot: Crown and Wisdom. The Light of Wisdom must

emerge from the Endless, PB''G (as explained above), and so the Light of Wisdom must traverse the Sefira of the Crown before it reaches the Sefira of Wisdom, and because the Light of Wisdom once shone in the Sefira of the Crown (when it traversed it), therefore it can never disappear from it (as explained above), and therefore it is necessary that even after the Light of Wisdom has reached the Sefira of Wisdom the Light of Wisdom still remains intact in the Crown. Thus the Sefira of Crown now has two Lights: the Light of the Crown, and the Light of Wisdom.

100) And so with the Light of Intelligence: since it must traverse the two preceding Sefirot before reaching the Sefira of Intelligence, it is of necessity that the Light of Intelligence obtained a place in the Crown and in Wisdom (as explained above). Now the Crown has three Lights: Light of Crown, Light of Wisdom, and Light of Intelligence. There are two Lights in the Sefira of Wisdom: Light of Wisdom and Light of Intelligence. There is one Light in the Sefira of Intelligence—its own. And so on, in like manner, until, with the emergence of the Light of the Kingdom, the Crown contains all ten sefirot, since all nine lower Lights have of necessity traversed the Crown, thereby obtaining a permanent place in it, as explained above. Wisdom has nine Sefirot, since all eight of the lower sefirot necessarily traversed it and in this manner remained fixed in it. Thus there are eight sefirot in Intelligence, seven in Mercy, six in Power, and so on, until Kingdom which contains its proper Light alone, since there is no Sefira below it to pass through on its way.

101) But the Light of the Kingdom—the Light it contains as well as the Light in the nine sefirot above it—is only Returning Light. We already know that from the time of the Contraction there came to be a Curtain in the Sefira of the Kingdom and the Light of the Endless is not received, but instead, when the Light of the Endless meets the Curtain, binding occurs— and a new Light emerges and ascends from the Curtain in the Kingdom, a light called Returning Light, which illumines up to the Sefira of the Crown and clothes from above to below all ten sefirot, and it is in this fashion that the Light of the Sefira Kingdom is found included in all of the first nine sefirot, as was asserted above. (*Inner Reflection*, volume II, 19, begin.: "From the meeting...").

102a) Since Kingdom is the source of this new Light, and every source is called Crown, Kingdom is considered the Sefira of Crown for the new Light, and the Sefira before it, which is Foundation, is considered as the Wisdom of the new Light, and the one before Foundation, which is Majesty, is considered as the Intelligence of the new Light; finally, the Upper Crown is considered the phase of Kingdom for the new Light from which it now receives.

102b) Thus we find that at each level of ten sefirot there are ten sefirot going in two directions. The first are the ten sefirot drawn from the Endless, PB''G, from above to below, from Crown to Kingdom, called Ten Sefirot of Straight Light, since they descend straightwise from above to below, in order of levels, i.e. from the purer vessel to the impurer, to the still impurer, down to the Kingdom, which is impurest of all.

103) There is, furthermore, a second set of ten sefirot which are drawn from the Kingdom from below to above, i.e. from the Sefira of the Kingdom to the Sefira of the Crown, with Kingdom serving as the source for this new light—these are the Ten Sefirot of Returning Light. They are called Returning Light because they operate opposite to the order of levels, that is to say they are not drawn and do not ascend from the purer Vessel to the impurer, with the last receiving Vessel being the impurest, but instead they are drawn and ascend from the impurest Vessel to the less impure Vessel, to the final receiving Vessel which is the purest; thus we speak of it illuminating from below to above.

104) As for the inclusiveness of the ten sefirot (which was explained above) regarding the Ten Sefirot of the Light of Straight Light: that, because there is no disappearance of Spiritual Substance, every illumination which traverses a Sefira remains there in its completeness, even when the illumination moves on to another place, and because of this all Ten Sefirot of Straight Light are included in the Crown, nine in Wisdom, eight in Intelligence, and so on (N.B. 99 above, begin.: "From what has been explained...")—for this very same reason we find a similar phenomenon in the Ten Sefirot of Returning Light. Since the Sefira of the Kingdom becomes the source for this Returning Light, each phase of the Returning Light which reaches a level above the Kingdom must pass through the Kingdom, for it is the Kingdom with its Curtain which emits the Returning Light when the Light of the Endless binds with the Curtain as a result of their meeting.

105) Therefore, when the Sefira of the Foundation receives the Returning Light from the Kingdom, it is of necessity that the Kingdom received this Light first by means of the binding with the Light of the Endless, passing through the Kingdom and reaching the Sefira of the Foundation, and so we find that the Light of the Foundation is to be found in both the Kingdom and the Foundation. Similarly, the Returning Light which the Sefira of Majesty receives necessarily obtained a place in both Kingdom and Foundation when traversing these Sefirot, and so the Kingdom now contains three Lights, the Foundation contains two, and the Majesty contains one. In this manner, when the last phase of the Returning Light has been received by the Crown, then the Kingdom has ten lights of Ten Sefirot of Returning Light, the Foundation has nine, Majesty eight, and so on, in a manner similar to the description of the Ten Sefirot of Straight Light.

106) Thus it turns out that there are ten Sefirot in each and every one of these ten Sefirot, i.e. including the Returning Light. In other words, the Light of the Kingdom received in each and every Sefira completes the number at ten, for the Crown has nine Sefirot of Straight Light: KH''B, HG''T, NH''Y, and one sefira of Returning Light: Kingdom, since it was the last Sefira to receive from the Ten Sefirot of Returning Light, as explained above, thus it receives only one light from the Returning Light.

107) Wisdom has eight Sefirot of Straight Light: H''B, HG''T, NH''Y, and two Sefirot from the Returning Light: first the portion of itself which it received from the Returning Light of the Kingdom, which is the Foundation of the Return-

ing Light, and second a portion of the Crown which passed through it, remaining and becoming Kingdom of the Returning Light, as explained above. Intelligence has seven Lights of Straight Light: Intelligence, HG"T, NH"Y, and three Sefirot from the Returning Light: Majesty, Foundation, and Kingdom. Majesty has its own, Foundation from the Wisdom which passed through it, and Kingdom from the Crown which passed through, i.e. from Intelligence and up (as explained above).

108) Mercy has six Sefirot of Straight Light: HG"T, NH"Y and four Sefirot of Returning Light, from Mercy and up: Lasting Endurance (of its own), and portions of Intelligence, Wisdom, and Crown, which are Majesty, Foundation, and Kingdom which passed through it and were fixed in it (as explained above). Similarly, Judgement has five Sefirot of Straight Light: Judgement, Beauty, Lasting Endurance, Majesty, and Foundations; and five of Returning Light, from Power and up: four portions of KHB"H, which are Lasting Endurance, Majesty, Foundation, and Kingdom which passed through it, and its own portion, which is Beauty of the Returning Light. Beauty has four Sefirot of Straight Light, from Beauty on down, and six Sefirot of Returning Light, from Beauty on up, i.e. five portions of KH"B, H"G, which are TNHY"M which passed through it, and its own portion which is Judgement of the Returning Light.

109) Lasting Endurance has three Sefirot of Straight Light, from Lasting Endurance on down: Lasting Endurance, Majesty, and Foundation of Straight Light, and seven Sefirot of Returning Light, from Lasting Endurance on up, which are

six portions of KH''B, HG''T which passed through it, which now are GTNHY''M, and its own portion, Mercy of the Returning Light. Majesty has two Sefirot of Straight Light: Majesty and Foundation, and eight Sefirot of Returning Light, from Majesty on up: seven portions of KH''B, HG''T and Lasting Endurance, which passed through it, and which are now HG''T, NHY''M of Returning Light, and its own portion, which is Intelligence of the Returning Light. Foundation has one Sefira of Straight Light, and nine Sefirot of Returning Light from Foundation on up, which are now eight portions of KH''B, HG''T, and N''H which passed through it and are now Intelligence HG''T, NHY''M of the Returning Light, and its own portion which is Wisdom of the Returning Light.

110) Thus it is clearly explained that in every revelation of ten Sefirot, wherever they may be, these Sefirot will be composed of one another; when the ten Sefirot of Straight Light emerge there is still lacking the Light of the Kingdom, i.e. Ten Sefirot of Returning Light—for this is the Kingdom's only light, and it completes the other Sefirot, bringing the number of Sefirot in each to ten.

111) If we take, for example, the Sefira of the Crown, which itself is composed of ten other Sefirot (i.e. after the Light of the Kingdom has been revealed in it), its first sefira which is Crown of the Crown is necessarily composed of nine Sefirot of Straight Light found below it: HBHG''TNH''Y of Straight Light in the Crown.

112) Even though only the Crown amongst them is original and the other nine Sefirot are not, but are lower lights which

have passed along, obtaining their places in passing from the Endless, PB''G, to Sefirot below the Crown, even so, because they are found in the Crown it is necessary that the highest Sefira among them, which is the secondary Crown, also includes nine tertiary Sefirot found below it, and these nine Sefirot, since they are found below it, must also have passed through it and must have obtained a place in it—since Spiritual Substance can not disappear (as explained above); thus this secondary Crown also contains ten Sefirot: nine Sefirot of Straightness: KH''B, HG''T, NH''Y, and one of Returning Light, which is Light of the Kingdom (as was true of its parent Crown).

113) In like manner, if we consider the secondary Wisdom of the ten secondary Sefirot of the primary Crown (Wisdom of Crown) one will necessarily find that it contains ten tertiary Sefirot (as explained above with regard to the secondary Crown), since all eight secondary Sefirot of the primary Crown of Straight Light found below it must necessarily have passed through it from above to below, and therefore obtained a place in it, and two Sefirot of Returning Light (from the light of the secondary Kingdom) also passed through it from below to above: its own Returning Light and the Returning Light belonging to the secondary Crown. Thus it too (the secondary Wisdom in the ten secondary Sefirot of the primary Crown) has ten Sefirot of its own, as does the primary Wisdom in the first set of ten Sefirot.

114) Similarly, if one examines the secondary Intelligence in the 10 secondary Sefirot of the primary Crown, which is called Intelligence of the Crown, one also finds that it neces-

sarily contains ten tertiary Sefirot as did the secondary Wisdom, for all 6 secondary Sefirot HG''T, NH''Y of the Straight Light of the primary Crown found below it necessarily passed through it from above to below, obtaining their places in it, being now, along with the Intelligence itself, 7 Sefirot of Straight Light. And 3 secondary Sefirot of Returning Light also passed through this Intelligence from the secondary Kingdom of the primary Crown from below to above i.e. a portion of its own Returning Light, a portion of the Returning Light of the secondary Wisdom, and a portion of the Returning Light of the secondary Crown—and so there are ten tertiary Sefirot in the secondary Intelligence of the Crown (first of the 10 primary Sefirot) as was the case with the primary Intelligence in the 10 primary Sefirot.

115) In like manner one finds 10 tertiary Sefirot in the secondary Sefirot of Mercy in the 10 secondary Sefirot of the primary Crown. They are: 6 of Straight Light HG''TNH''Y, from above to below, and four of Returning Light from Mercy on up to the Crown. In a similar manner one finds 10 tertiary Sefirot in Judgement and so on, until the secondary Kingdom of the 10 secondary Sefirot which is called Kingdom of the Crown.

116) One may not question the fact that the 10 secondary Sefirot of the primary Crown contain only the phase of Life from the Returning Light which ascended from the primary Kingdom, i.e. the last part of the Returning Light, smallest of all 10 Sefirot of the Returning Light (as explained above, see 112, begin.: "Even though...") and so how can it be said that this small portion of the Returning Light now spreads

itself into 10 new Sefirot of Returning Light so as to complete for each secondary Sefira the tertiary Sefirot which are lacking their tenth Sefira?

117) The answer is that, ultimately, that part of the Life of the secondary Returning Light which ascended from the Kingdom to the primary Crown necessarily sufficed to clothe all 9 secondary Sefirot found in the primary Crown, for if this were not the case then these 9 Sefirot of Straight Light would not reach and illumine the Countenance at all, for the Straight Light has no way of reaching the Countenance, save by means of the Vessel of Receival in the Returning Light, and since this Light of the Life clothed the 9 secondary Sefirot in the Crown then it must follow that in passing from below to above it completed each and every one of the tertiary Sefirot for the ten secondary Sefirot. Thus to Wisdom it gave 2 missing Lights: one in the actual clothing, one on its way to clothe the Crown; to Intelligence it gave 3, and to Mercy 4, as explained above.

118) Just as the ten tertiary Sefirot of the 10 secondary Sefirot of the primary Crown are explained, so may be explained the 10 tertiary Sefirot of each and every one of the secondary Sefirot of the primary Sefira of Wisdom. For in the Crown of the 10 secondary Sefirot of the primary Wisdom, called the Crown of Wisdom, one of necessity finds 10 tertiary Sefirot: its own secondary Light, 8 secondary Sefirot—H''B HG''T NH''Y which passed through it from above to below, (which gives us 9 so far), and one Returning Light which ascended from the secondary Kingdom of the primary Wis-

dom—and so in all there are 10 tertiary Sefirot in the Crown of the primary Sefira of Wisdom.

119) So with the secondary Sefira of Wisdom amongst the 10 secondary Sefirot of the primary Wisdom (called Wisdom of Wisdom) we find 8 Sefirot of Straight Light from above to below, and 2 Sefirot of Returning Light from below to above. And so with the secondary Sefira of Intelligence amongst the ten secondary Sefirot of the primary Sefira of Wisdom, we find 7 Sefirot of Straight Light from above to below, and 3 Sefirot of Returning Light from below to above, and so on with Mercy, Judgement, etc. up to the secondary Kingdom in the 10 Sefirot of the primary Wisdom called Kingdom of Wisdom which also contains 10 tertiary Sefirot of Returning Light, i.e. by virtue of the fact that it clothes of necessity all 10 secondary Sefirot of the primary Wisdom, sending them its illumination whereby all of them necessarily have passed through it obtaining a place in it.

120) In a similar way the 10 tertiary Sefirot of the secondary Intelligence are distinguished. And so the secondary Sefira of Mercy, and the secondary Sefira of Judgement, and so on, up until the secondary Sefira of Kingdom—there is no need to elaborate further. Instead we shall explain one tertiary Sefira to demonstrate how it too is necessarily composed of 10 quaternary Sefirot.

121) If we take the tertiary Intelligence, one of the tertiary Sefirot found for example in the secondary Wisdom of the 10 secondary Sefirot of the primary Sefira of Wisdom, (called Intelligence of Wisdom of Wisdom) we find that it too con-

tains 10 Sefirot, as do the Sefirot discussed above, i.e. 7 of Straight Light, which passed through it from above to below and 3 of Returning Light which passed through it from below to above.

122) And so one can continue to analyze the Sefirot *ad infinitum* for any Sefira, even at the thousandth remove, will be found to have been passed through by the other Sefirot, some from above to below, some from below to above, thereby obtaining an eternal place in the Sefira in question—thus every Sefira contains all 10 Sefirot—understand this well.

123) However the reader must realize that even though the Sefirot consist of 10 Sefirot within each individual Sefira, *ad infinitum*, still and all they are not all equal, but instead they go through many changes in their extension, one Sefira *not* being the same as another. For, in every case except the Crown, the Lights of Straight Light do not come in their normal place. Thus, in the Sefira of Wisdom one finds only 8 Lights of Straight Light, from Wisdom on down, and 2 Lights of Returning Light, Foundation and Kingdom, and so the 8 Lights of Straight Light came to the purest Vessels, from Crown to Majesty and the 2 Lights of Returning Light in Foundation and Kingdom. Thus the Light of Wisdom comes to the Vessel of Crown, the Light of Intelligence in the Vessel of Wisdom, etc., until the Light of Foundation which comes to the Vessel of Majesty. It is the Lights of Straight Light which all arrive out of place, and only the Returning Light which always arrives at the right place, for the Returning Light of Foundation arrives in the Vessel of Foundation and

the Returning Light of Kingdom in the Vessel appropriate to the Kingdom of Kingdom.

124) And so with Intelligence which has only 7 Lights of Straight Light. These Lights are received in the purest Vessels, since as stated above, any receiver does so in the purest Vessel it has—in this case, from Crown to Lasting Endurance, and so the Light of Intelligence is received by the Vessel of the Crown and the Light of Mercy in Wisdom, and so on until the Light of the Foundation in the Vessel of Lasting Endurance. It is only the 3 Lights of Returning Light which arrive in their proper place: Majesty, Foundation, and Kingdom in the Vessels of Majesty, Foundation, and Kingdom.

125) From the above one will understand that there is a great difference between the secondary Intelligence of the Crown and the secondary Intelligence of Wisdom, and between the secondary Intelligence of Intelligence and so on, for Intelligence of the Crown has the Light of Intelligence in its Vessel, and this is not true of Intelligence of Wisdom where in fact the Light of Mercy is in the Vessel of Intelligence. As for Intelligence of Intelligence, it has the Light of Power in the Vessel of Intelligence and the same holds true for the other Sefirot, no two being alike.

126) Even the Lights of the Returning Light, which do not enter Vessels other than their own, undergo changes in their extension, as a result of its illumination by the Straight Light. Thus, for example, Foundation of Wisdom is illumined by the Straight Light of Majesty of Wisdom, however Foundation of Intelligence is illumined by Lasting Endurance of In-

telligence, for Majesty of Intelligence has no Straight Light, as explained above.

127) An exception to this rule holds true if we examine the primary Sefira alone; what I mean is if you take, for example, the primary Sefira of Intelligence and examine its tertiary Sefirot of Intelligence, called the Sefira of Intelligence of Intelgence of Intelligence, one finds all these Sefirot are equal; and one finds in all of them 7 Lights of Straight Light in the 7 highest Vessels: KH"B HG"T and Lasting Endurance, and 3 Lights of Returning Light in the 3 lowest Vessels: Majesty, Foundation, Kingdom. The same will hold true of even the thousandth Intelligence of Intelligence of Intelligence—likewise for the remaining Sefirot.

CHAPTER 10

BINDING BY STRIKING

Explaining: The matter of Binding by Striking which includes two powers: drawing and pushing, both operative at the same time. One operates in the impurity and the other in the hardness of the Curtain.

A lengthy Explanation dealing with the Meaning of the Words: Binding by Striking.

128) The matter of Binding by Striking referred to above requires a lengthy explanation, for we have here apparently positive and negative qualities at the same time. For Binding implies drawing, adherence, and love whereas Striking implies pushing, separation, and great hate—how can one speak of Binding by Striking? It is like speaking of a hateful love or an adherence or a drawing that is a pushing away. Indeed, it seems unimaginable.

129) But the truth is that these are two opposites under one power which is composed of two distinct parts, i.e. two distinct powers: a drawing power and a pushing power. The drawing power resides in the impurity of the Vessel and the pushing power resides in the Curtain in the Vessel, both of which are compounded and each of which operates at the same time in two places.

130) To make this perfectly clear, without causing any doubt or confusion, I shall expand this explanation a bit. Let us take a familiar example from the material universe as an analogy. When one sees a stone or a man fall to the ground from a high place it appears to the eye that the man is drawn downwards with great force and speed, and yet when he reaches the ground he is struck and pushed upwards somewhat by it.

131) There are two opinions regarding this example: according to one the globe exerts a great pull on everything in the air, which has no solid mass supporting it. Therefore when the man is removed from the roof of the house into the air, then the pull of the earth at once effects him. This accounts for the rapidity of his fall to the ground. Yet according to this view one would expect that the earth would embrace him, as it were, with great love, without allowing him to move from it whatsoever, for even a moment. We find, instead, that the opposite is true, for the moment he touches it he is at once pushed back upwards a bit.

132) Against this opinion there is another which holds that there is some power which pushes from above the air of our earth, and this power operates on every object found in the air, pushing it to the ground. The earth itself also has a pushing power (not a drawing power), and so when the man is removed from the roof of the house and is in the air the pushing power at once begins to operate from above, forcing him down, and when he reaches the ground it in turn pushes him back up.

133) But if we compare the branch to its root in the Upper Worlds (for there are, most often, resemblances between the two, we find that both of these opinions are wrong, and one may add here, that every globe has drawing and pushing powers which are combined with one another, i.e. they contain a power of impurity which is the power to draw in whatever is outside, and a power of hardness which pushes away every external body preventing its entry. Therefore all power of drawing emanates from the interior Middle Point where the drawing power resides, this being the thickest point in the entire globe, for which reason it draws everything in the surrounding void which comes under its power and influence.

134) Nevertheless it does not draw an object to consume it, as it would have were it only for its power of drawing— but at the moment the object drawn touches the outermost layer of the drawing object, at once the pushing power which inheres the hard surface is awakened and pushes the object back up.

135) Thus, that which it draws is not received by the drawing, for it is stopped in mid-course by the power of hardness which pushes and prevents the drawn object (as explained above)—since Binding and Striking are operating here at the same time. The Binding power draws and the hardness repels, so that the object reaches the outer surface but is not swallowed up. Thus one might say that the essence of the Vessel of Receival is the pushing power which receives and holds the object as it should, for without it the object would be swallowed up.

136) One will also take note that the drawing and pushing powers are equal, like two drops of water. For if the drawing power were somewhat greater than the pushing power then it would be impossible for an object to hover, for it would be drawn in as iron is drawn in by a magnet; if the pushing power were greater, then all of existence would dance about it, unable to approach—thus the two powers must be equal.

137) One may therefore well understand the Binding by Striking which operates in the Upper Worlds. Even though Binding and Striking are antithetical, they still operate at the same time under the same power, but in two places: the impurity (thickness) and the hardness. Remember this to facilitate your understanding of the Wisdom of the Kabbalah which follows.

TABLE OF VOCABULARY QUESTIONS

1. What is Primordial Man?
2. What is Returning Light?
3. What is Straight Light?
4. What is Surrounding Light?
5. What is Inner Light?
6. What is Length?
7. What is Intelligence?
8. What is Not Joined?
9. What is Boundary?
10. What is Roof?
11. What is Body?
12. What is Wheel?
13. What are the Three First (Sefirot) (G"R)?
14. What is Corporeality?
15. In Passing?
16. Illumination from Afar?
17. Purification of the Curtain?
18. Absolute farness?
19. What is Bowing of the Head?
20. What is Inclusiveness of the Sefirot?
21. What is Binding?
22. What is One within the Other?
23. What is Binding by Striking?
24. What is The Small Face (Z"A)?

25. What are the Seven Lower (Sefirot) (Z''T)?
26. What is Material?
27. What is Living?
28. What is Outer, or exteriority?
29. What is Wisdom?
30. What is Window?
31. What is Individual?
32. What is Emergence?
33. What is Descent?
34. What is Straight?
35. What is Crown?
36. What is Slowly, or bit by bit?
37. What is Binder?
38. What are Waters of Light?
39. What is Kingdom?
40. What is From Above to Below?
41. What is From Below to Above?
42. Cause?
43. Curtain?
44. Surrounding?
45. Nullified?
46. Drawn?
47. Life?
48. NRNH''Y?
49. Soul?
50. Encircling?
51. What is Conclusion?
52. What is Near?

53. What is Thickness or Impurity?
54. What is Passing?
55. What are Upper and Lower?
56. What is Essence or Substance?
57. What is Inner, or Interiority?
58. What are Inner and Outer, or Interiority and Exteriority?
59. What is Pipe?
60. What is Line?
61. What is Erect Height?
62. What is Edge?
63. What is Ground?
64. What is Head?
65. What is Spirit?
66. Spirituality?
67. Far?
68. Beginning of Extension?
69. What is At Once?
70. What is the End and Purpose of all the Above?

TABLE OF TOPICAL QUESTIONS

71. What is the source of the Vessels of the Circles?
72. What are the Impressions left in the Circles after the Restriction?
73. Why are the Circles one within the other?
74. Why is there no (attribute) phase of one within the other in the Endless, PB"G?
75. What is the root of all the Lights?
76. What is the root of all the Vessels?
77. What is the source of the Returning Light?
78. Why do the Lights precede the Vessels?
79. Why does Intelligence not precede Wisdom?
80. What is the source of the Power of Control in the Worlds?
81. Where is the Curtain drawn from?
82. How many causes preceded the Curtain?
83. What is the source of the Vessels of Straightness?
84. From where do the Circles receive Light?
85. How do the Circles receive Light one from the other?
86. Why must the Circles receive (Light) from Straightness?
87. What are the Windows in the Roof and Floor of every Circle?
88. What caused the Circles to be one below the other?
89. Why do the Circles require that the Line join them together?
90. What is the difference between Sefirot of Straightness and Sefirot of Circles?

91. Why is the Power of Restriction not sufficient, and the Curtain also necessary?

92. What are Lights of Straightness?

93. What is the difference between straight Illumination and Circling Illumination?

94. In what way are the Circles superior to Straightness?

95. In what way are the Sefirot of Straightness superior to those of the Circles?

96. Why is every exterior Circle superior to others more interior?

97. Why do the Interior Vessels of Straightness surpass the others?

98. Why is the World of Making (Action) exterior to all the other Worlds?

99. What caused the emergence of the Curtain?

100. When was the Curtain made?

101. Why does the ascent of the Curtain depend on the extent of impurity in the fourth phase?

102. What are the Vessels of Receival in the Light of the Line?

103. What are the two kinds of Ten Sefirot in every Emanation?

104. Why is the Returning Light considered a Vessel of Receival?

105. What determines the size of the Returning Light?

106. Why is Kingdom distinguished as the Crown of the Returning Light?

107. Why do the Curtain and the Impurity act as one?

108. Why do the Impurity and the Returning Light depend one upon the other?

109. What purifies the Curtain?

110. Why are the Sefirot of the Circles in the phase of Life?
111. Why are the Sefirot of Straightness in the phase of Spirit?
112. What is the attribute of the first three Sefirot of Straightness?
113. How do the Sefirot of Straightness stand within the Circles?
114. Why do the Circles stand in the place of the first three Sefirot of Straightness?
115. What is the distance from Circle to Circle?
116. Why do the Circles not encircle the 7 lower Sefirot of Straightness?
117. Why is it forbidden to deal with the first 3 Sefirot of each Level?
118. Is it forbidden to deal with all of the ten secondary Sefirot of the first 3 Sefirot?
119. Why do we not deal with the Sefirot of the Circles?
120. How do the 10 Sefirot divide according to the five phases of Desire?
121. What is the meaning of "exactly 10," not nine, not eleven?
122. Why is the Desire to Receive not revealed all at once?
123. Why is Impurity considered Interior?
124. Why is specifically the Interior considered a Vessel of Receival?
125. What determines the largeness or smallness of the Worlds?
126. Why did the Light withdraw from the first 3 phases as well at the time of the Restriction?
127. What are the three aspects of the Vessels?
128. What are the two aspects of Spiritual substances?

129. Until what time is the Emanation considered as the Upper?

130. When is the Emanation considered to leave the Upper for its own domain?

131. What is the meaning of Not Possible?

132. What is the meaning of Not Intending?

133. Why is phase 1 distinguished as Not Possible, and Not Intending?

134. Why is phase 2 distinguished as Possible, and Not Intending?

135. Why is phase 3 distinguished as Not Possible and Intending?

136. Why is phase 4 distinguished as Possible and Intending?

137. Why are not all phases of the Desire worthy of Vessels of Receival, merely phase 4?

138. Why does every change of form in the impurity of phase 4 emerge as an attribute of a new Emanation?

139. Why doesn't the Upper Light leave off from the Emanations for even a moment?

140. What is the difference between Influence and Receival in the Vessels?

141. Why is Influence exerted over the more Impure and Receival over the more Pure?

142. How are we to understand Renewal of Form as the Upper Light is extended?

143. How does an Emanation emerge from the Upper Light?

144. What is the difference between the names of the 4 phases and the names KH"BZ"N.

145. What is the order of entrance of Lights into the Emanation after the Restoration?

146. What is the order of the growth of the Vessels in each Countenance after the Restoration?

147. What is the first substance of each Emanation?

148. What are the two Crowns at each level?

149. Why doesn't the Light disappear from one place as it passes to another?

150. In what way is every Upper Sefira comprised of those below it?

151. In what way is every Lower Sefira comprised of those above it?

152. What is the key to finding distinctions between Sefirot comprised of one another?

153. What are the phases of Straight Light and Returning Light found in Crown?

154. What are the phases of Straight Light and Returning Light found in Wisdom?

155. What are the phases of Straight Light and Returning Light found in Intelligence?

156. What are the phases of Straight Light and Returning Light found in Mercy?

157. What are the phases of Straight Light and Returning Light found in Judgement?

158. What are the phases of Straight Light and Returning Light found in Beauty?

159. What are the phases of Straight Light and Returning Light found in Lasting Endurance?

160. What are the phases of Straight Light and Returning Light found in Majesty?

161. What are the phases of Straight Light and Returning Light found in Foundation?

162. What are the phases of Straight Light and Returning Light found in Kingdom?

163. What are the phases of Straight Light and Returning Light found in Crown of the Crown?

164. What are the phases of Straight Light and Returning Light found in Wisdom of the Crown?

165. What are the phases of Straight Light and Returning Light found in Intelligence of the Crown?

166. What are the phases of Straight Light and Returning Light found in Mercy of the Crown of the Crown?

167. What are the phases of Straight Light and Returning Light found in Judgement of Wisdom of Lasting Endurance?

168. What are the phases of Straight Light and Returning Light found in Beauty of Intelligence of Majesty?

169. What are the phases of Straight Light and Returning Light found in Lasting Endurance of Foundation of Crown?

170. What are the phases of Straight Light and Returning Light found in Majesty of Beauty of Kingdom?

171. How are the Lights of Straightness and Returning Light clothed in the Vessels?

172. What is the order of cause and effect from the Endless, Praised Be God, to the Kingdom of Primordial Man?

TABLE OF ANSWERS
TO VOCABULARY QUESTIONS

1. *Primordial Man* (volume 2, part 1, *Inner Light*, V): This is the first World which receives from the Endless, Praised Be God, also called a Single Line, drawn immediately after the Restriction, from the Endless, PB"G, up until this World. The term "Man" refers only to the Sefirot of the Straightness in the First World, which is Light of Spirit, which means a Light which influences, it does not refer to the Sefirot of Circles in the First World, since they have only Light of Life, which means a Light which receives, without the ability to influence by itself. This is the Root of the phase of Man in this World.

2. *Returning Light* (volume 2, *Inner Reflection*, 79): This is the Light which is not received in phase four. In other words, this is the sole light to fill the fourth phase without being received in it, on account of the Curtain which prevents it and turns it backwards. This action is termed Binding by Striking (see *Inner Reflection*, volume 2, 22, begin.: "It has been..."). All Vessels of Receival in the Countenances, from the Restriction onwards, are drawn from this Returning Light which serves them instead of the fourth phase which is in the Endless, PB"G.

3. *Straight Light* (volume 2, *Inner Reflection*, 94): This is the Upper Light drawn from the Endless, PB"G, and influenced in the Countenances, from the Restriction onwards.

It is termed thus to indicate that it is not influenced by the Vessels of Circles, likewise with all levels not having any of the impurity of the fourth phase, except for the Sefirot of Straightness alone, following the rule that influence may be exerted only on something more impure, this being the Impurity in the fourth phase.

4. *Surrounding Light* (volume 2, part 1, *Inner Light*, M): This is the Light appointed to be clothed in a level but which is prevented by some boundary in it. The name has 2 meanings: first, that it is Illumination at a distance; second, that it is a certain Illumination, in other words, that ultimately it is destined to be clothed there, since the Light "surrounds" from all sides not leaving any room for escape, until worthy of complete Receival.

5. *Inner Light* (volume 2, part 1, *Inner Light*, M): This is the Light clothed in the Vessel.

6. *Length* (volume 2, part 2, *Inner Light*, Dv, begin.: "This means from..."): The distance between the 2 limits of a level, in other words, the distance from the purest phase to the impurest phase is termed "length," the same is true of analagous material length which refers to the distance between the upper edge and the lower edge.

7. *Intelligence* (volume 2, part 1, *Inner Light*, T): Reflection on the ways of cause and effect in order to clarify all of anything's results is termed "Intelligence."

8. *Not Joined* (volume 2, 3): Equivalence of form between 2 Spiritual Substances is Juncture; change in their forms, causes them to be "not joined," one to the other.

9. *Boundary* (volume 2, *Inner Reflection*, 79): The Curtain at each level stretches out and makes a "Boundary" at that level at the height of the Returning Light which the Curtain sends up (see above §2) according to its impurity, for the Curtain of Phase 3 limits the height of the level to prevent it from reaching the Light of the Crown. The Curtain of Phase 2 limits it also from the Light of Wisdom, etc.

10. *Roof* (volume 2, part 1, *Inner Light*, Av): This is the Crown at each level. This holds true for both Sefirot and Worlds.

11. *Body* (volume 2, part 1, *Inner Light*, R): True Vessels of Receival at each level which spread out by virtue of the power of the Returning Light in the Curtain, from the Curtain downwards, are called the "Body" of the level, since they precede the Lights. Contrast with this the Lights which extend for the purpose of Binding by Striking with the Curtain—these Lights precede the Vessels.

12. *Wheel* (volume 2, 2): Sefirot of Circles are termed "Wheels," since the Lights circle within them, in other words, it is impossible to distinguish purity or impurity within them.

13. *The First Three* (volume 2, part 1, *Inner Light*, R): These are Lights which preceded the Vessels, clothed in the Returning Light which ascends to them from the Curtain and upwards. They are the first three Sefirot: Crown, Wisdom, and Intelligence, also called the Head of the Countenance.

14. *Corporeality*: Anything preceived with the five senses, or occupying time and space, is termed "Corporeality."

15. *In Passing* (volume 2, part 1, *Inner Light*, Dv): The Lights drawn from the Endless, PB''G, to the Lower Sefirot necessarily pass through the Upper Sefirot and since Spiritual Substance does not disappear from Place A when it passes to Place B, surviving instead in both A and B, therefore we distinguish in each Sefira 2 kinds of Lights: Lights proper to the phase of the Sefira, and Lights remaining there "in passing."

16. *Illumination from Afar* (volume 2, part 1, *Inner Light*, M): The type of illumination at work in the Countenance when the Countenance does not have vessels of Receival for its Light is called "Illumination from Afar"; meaning that there is distance and significant change between the Light and the Vessels of the Countenance related to that Light. Thus the Vessels are not capable of receiving that Light, and enclothing it, instead they are illuminated by it from afar.

17. *Purification of the Curtain* (volume 2, *Inner Reflection*, 74): This is purification of the impurity in the fourth phase. Since the height of the Returning Light, which the Curtain sends up and clothes the Straight Light with, depends on the amount of impurity in phase four (see above §2, Returning Light)—that is the amount of longing in phase 4—thus after the level has been filled with the Light that it has drawn, the surrounding Light then exerts itself to purify the Curtain, according to whatever the amount of longing there is. We term this purification from the impurities which were within it, also called "Purification of the Curtain."

18. *Absolute Farness* (volume 2, B): When the change in form is so great as to become an opposition of form, from one end to the other, this is termed "Absolute Farness."

19. *Bowing of the Head* (volume 2, part 2, *Inner Light*, C): When the Lights of the Seven Lower Sefirot serve also in the head, called the first 3 Sefirot, since the Lights of the first three Sefirot which belong to the Head are lacking there this we term "Bowing of the Head." In other words, the Head is lowered to a level equal to that of the 7 lower Sefirot, those called Body.

20. *Inclusiveness of the Sefirot* (volume 2, *Inner Reflection*, 97): The Sefirot include one another "in passing" (see above answer 16). Since the 10 Sefirot of the Light of Straightness drawn from the Crown to the Kingdom are unable to appear at a level without being clothed in 10 Sefirot of the Returning Light, drawn and assembled from Kingdom to Crown thus there is not a single Sefira among them which does not contain 2 Sefirot in itself: one of Straight Light and one of Returning Light. Furthermore, 8 other Sefirot are included in passing, some having passed from above to below, and some having passed from below to above.

21. *Binding* (volume 2, part 1, *Inner Light*, K): The enclothing of the 10 sefirot of the Head level in the 10 Sefirot of the Returning Light which ascend from Kingdom from below to above—this is termed "Binding." The reason for this is that the Lights precede the Vessels, for impurity does not ascend whatsoever with this Returning Light higher than its proper place, which is Kingdom. Therefore, the 10 Sefirot of the Re-

turning Light are not considered complete Vessels worthy of the enclothing of substance in them. Therefore, this type of enclothing is merely termed Binding, in other words, the Straight Light binds with and dwells upon the Countenance by means of these 10 Sefirot of Returning Light even though it doesn't actually clothe itself within them. We speak of the enclothing of Straight Light within the Vessels only with respect to the Returning Light which spreads downwards from the Curtain, whereby the impurity of the Kingdom of the Head is able to extend, spread, and descend and clothe the ten Sefirot of Straight Light which enter it.

22. *One within the Other* (volume 2, part 2, *Inner Light*, M): This means one causes the other; for an outer Circle is defined as the cause of the Circle within it, caused by and drawn from the outer in such a way that "one within the other" points to the relationship of "cause and effect" that exists between them.

23. *Binding by Striking* (volume 2, *Inner Reflection*, 18): The action of the Curtain which hinders and hides the Light from the fourth phase pushing it instead backwards to its Root— this action is called "Binding by Striking." The form of the term indicates that the action contains 2 opposite aspects: on the one hand it "strikes" the Light which means that it pushes and deflects it, not allowing it to illuminate; on the other hand there is "binding" with the Light which means that it causes an increase and expansion, for, indeed, the amount of Light hidden and pushed away from the fourth phase becomes the great revealed Light which enclothes the Straight Light, called Returning Light without which it is absolutely impossible for

the Light of the Endless, PB''G, to be clothed in the Countenance.

24. *The Small Face, Z''A* (volume 2, *Inner Reflection*, 13): The Small Face means literally a "small face," for the Light of Wisdom is termed "Light of the Face" which is the secret meaning of the verse "A man's wisdom lights his face"; similarly, the Countenance of the Crown in the World of Emanation "The Long Face" which means "A large face" because its essence is the Light of Wisdom. Therefore the third phase whose essence is merely the Light of Mercy drawn from Intelligence (also containing however, illumination from Wisdom without its essence being the Light of Wisdom) is termed because of this a small face, which is to say, "The Small Face," for the Light of its Face is decreased and diminished compared to the first phase.

25. *Z''T, The Seven Lower Sefirot* (volume 2, part 1, *Inner Light*, R): The 10 Sefirot drawn from the Curtain and downwards are termed Body or "Z''T" (see above, answer 11). Insofar as the entire Countenance is sometimes distinguished into 10 Sefirot alone, the first 3 Sefirot will be Crown, Wisdom, and Intelligence in the Head of the Countenance and the 7 lower Sefirot which are Mercy, Judgement, Beauty, Lasting Endurance, Majesty, Foundation and Kingdom will be in the Body of the Countenance.

26. *Material* (volume 2, *Inner Reflection*, 40): The impurity in the Countenance from the fourth phase of the Desire (see ahead, "Impurity," §53), is termed "Material" of the Countenance. This term is analagous to matter in a physical sense,

it too having 3 dimensions, length, breadth and depth and 6 directions above, below, east, west, north, south.

27. *Living* (volume 2, part 2, *Inner Light*, F): This is the Light of Wisdom as in the secret meaning of the verse "Wisdom shall give life to her possessor."

28. *Outer* (volume 2, *Inner Reflection*, 6): The purer part of each Vessel is distinguished as the "outer" of the Vessel, and this is the phase of the Vessel for the surrounding Light which illumines it from afar.

29. *Wisdom* (volume 2, part 1, *Inner Light*, T): Knowledge of the final ends of all the manifold aspects of Reality is called "Wisdom."

30. *Window* (volume 2, part 2, *Inner Light*, P): The power from the impurity of the Curtain distinguished by 10 Sefirot of the Head of a level or 10 Sefirot of Circles, this same power of impurity which functions with the Returning Light which ascends from the Curtain is called "Window." This means the Returning Light pushed from the fourth phase because of its impurity becomes a Vessel of Receival for the Upper Light instead of the fourth phase which was a Vessel of Receival in the Endless, PB"G. The reason for this is that the Returning Light really comprises, the impurity of the fourth phase keeping it with it in its descent from the Endless, PB"G (see Inner Reflection, volume 2, §29, begin.: "The rule is..."). However, this impurity is merely recognizable in the Vessels of the Body since they extend from below the Curtain, that is to say from below the fourth phase of the 10 Sefirot of the Head—thus the impurity of the fourth phase of the Curtain holds sway

over them; they are therefore considered complete Vessels for the clothing of the Upper Light. This is not the case with the 10 Sefirot of the Head which are necessarily above their fourth phase. Instead, the Returning Light ascends to them from below to above and the impurity of the fourth phase of the Curtain is unable to be included with and to ascend with the Returning Light above its normal place to the nine Sefirot which precede it; therefore, this Returning Light does not then become Vessels of Receival but merely Roots for Vessels of Receival alone. This is why the enclothing of the 9 Sefirot in this Returning Light is called only Binding (see above §21). At the same time, with respect to the 9 Sefirot of the Head the Returning Light is distinguished as "the potential of Impurity," for it becomes the potential of Binding able to seize the Emanation. This potential is termed "Window," because when the Returning Light and the Straight Light enter to illuminate the pure Vessels of the Circles which do not possess the least bit of impurity the power of impurity in the Returning Light is far lower than the power of impurity in the Vessels and so it lowers the walls of the Vessels of the Circles "in the course of entering them." Compare the hole in a room which is a "lack in the wall of the room, however it is the path through which sunlight enters. Similarly the lack created in the walls of the Vessels of the Circles by the power of impurity in the Returning Light is not really considered a fault but a window, for without it they would not have any Light. For they only receive Light by way of the Line through the power of its Curtain.

31. *Individual* (volume 2, part 2, *Inner Light*, F): Light clothed in the Sefira of the Crown is called "Individual."

32. *Emergence to the Exterior* (volume 2, *Inner Reflection,* 59): A change in the form of Spiritual Substance is termed "emergence to the exterior." Thus a change in the form of a part of the Countenance means that a part of the Countenance emerged from the Countenance outwards. Compare the Lighting of a candle with another candle, the first not losing anything, for there is no disappearance of Spiritual Substance. Thus we find that when a part begins to change its form it also begins to separate from the Countenance and to emerge outside the Countenance to a new domain of its own. Therefore, change in form, and "emergence to the exterior" are the same thing.

33. *Descent* (volume 2, part 1, *Inner Light,* Ev): Impurification (thickening) means "descent," in other words descent from a level. Purification means ascent for there has been "an ascent" in the resemblance of the form to the Endless, PB"G; the rule is: the purer is the higher, the impurer (thicker) is the lower.

34. *Straight* (volume 2, part 1, *Inner Light,* E): When the Upper Light descends to Vessels having the impurity of the fourth phase, which means longing, since it continues the light in its Longing, we describe Light's descent as "straight," in other words, directly proportional to the amount of impurity and longing in it. Compare a heavy object which falls to the ground from a height—it falls in a straight line, swiftly, because of the earth's pull on it. This is not the case with something light, on which the earth's pull doesn't work, which floats slowly to the ground. Thus here: Vessels without impurity, such as Vessels of Circles, whose Light comes to them

by the Power of Sefirot of Straightness—their Light becomes circular, since there is no impurity there, i.e. Longing to draw the Light with its pull. This is not the case with Vessels of Straightness which possess impurity that draws the Light with great power, causing the Light to descend swiftly and with exact straightness, similar to a "Straight" line.

35. *Crown* (volume 2, part 1, *Inner Light*, T): The supervision of the Root on the level is called Crown, from the word "crowning" which means surrounding. Since it is the purest of all levels it is found to surround the entire Countenance from above.

36. *Slowly* (volume 2, part 1, *Inner Light*, F): The drawing of Lights in order of levels, in the order of cause and effect, is termed "slowly."

37. *Binder* (volume 2, part 1, *Inner Light*, L): The Kingdom of an Upper Sefira becomes the Crown of a lower, thus each Kingdom "binds" every upper Sefira with that below it; in other words, an equality of form is established between them. In this manner a "connection" is established between all the levels, from the World of Primordial Man to the end of the World of Action. This holds true for the Vessels of Straightness called Line, and not for the Vessels of Circles. Therefore, every connection of Circles one to the other is brought about by the Line.

38. *Waters of Light* (volume 2, part 1, *Inner Light*, D): The Light which descends from its level is termed water or "waters of Light."

39. *Kingdom* (volume 2, part 1, *Inner Light*, T): The last phase is called "Kingdom" because from it is drawn an attribute of strict control analagous to the fear of an actual earthly Kingdom.

40. *From above to below* (volume 2, *Inner Reflection*, 102B): Light which extends in the Vessels from level to level, from pure to impure is termed "from above to below." This light is called Straight Light.

41. *From below to above* (volume 2, *Inner Reflection*, 103): Light drawn in order of levels from impure to pure to purest is called "from below to above." This Light is called Returning Light.

42. *Cause*: That which brings about the revelation of a level is said to cause it as in "cause and effect," for cause means that which brings something about and effect means that which is brought about by its cause.

43. *Curtain* (volume 3, part 1, 2): "Power of Restriction," awakened in the Emanation with respect to the Upper Light, stopping it in its downward descent to the fourth phase, that is to say the moment the Light reaches and touches the fourth phase this power is immediately awakened, striking and pushing the Light backwards—it is this power which is called "Curtain." We must clearly distinguish between the Curtain in the Emanation and its Restriction, for they are two totally different things—for the Power of Restriction in the fourth phase operates with respect to the Vessel in the Emanation being a longing to receive which means that on account of the Desire for equality of form to the Emanator it prevented

itself from receiving at the time of its longing to receive. For the longing within it which is called the fourth phase is an upper power which the Emanation is not able to do away with or to decrease, but it is instead able to prevent itself from Desiring to Receive even though its longing is great. This power of prevention rests always with the fourth phase of the Emanation, except when it is drawing new Light, for then it must do away with the power of prevention (which is its Restriction) revealing its longing for the Upper Light, whereby its power is able to draw the Light to itself. At this point beings the working of the Curtain in the Emanation, for all longing draws the Upper Light in its entirety (as it was in the Endless, PB''G), since it is an upper power, no lower power being able to decrease it, as explained above. Thus the Light descends to fill the fourth phase. However, at the moment when the Light touches the fourth phase, the Curtain is at once awakened, striking the Light and returning it backwards—thus only the Light of 3 phases is received, the fourth phase not receiving. It is apparent therefore that the Curtain functions only at the arrival of the Light (after the Power of Restriction has been done away) in order to draw new Light, as explained. But the function of Restriction is permanent, preventing itself from drawing Light. Thus Restriction and Curtain are 2 phases totally different from one another, Curtain being an off-spring of Restriction.

44. *Surrounding* (volume 2, part 1, *Inner Light*, M): See Answer 4.

45. *Nullified* (volume 2, part 1, *Inner Light*, J): When 2 Spiritual Substances are exactly equal in form, without any

differences whatsoever, they return to one substance, the smaller being "nullified" in the larger.

46. *Drawn* (volume 2, part 1, *Inner Light*, R): The descent of Light by the power of impurity, which means the power of longing in the Emanation, is called "drawn" or drawing.

47. *Life* (volume 2, *Inner Reflection*, 95): Light which does not come to the Countenance through the Light of the End-less, PB"G, but is received instead from the next highest level is called Light of Life or Female Light.

48. *NRNH"Y* (volume 2, *Inner Reflection*, 87): Vessels in the 10 Sefirot are called KH"B,Z"N. The Lights in the 10 Sefirot are called "Life, Spirit, Soul, Living, Individual." The reason for their being named from first to last, that is to say NRNH"Y instead of from last to first, that is to say YHNR"N, is because the former represents their order of entry into the Countenance: first Life, then Spirit etc. This is the opposite of what holds true for the Vessels, where Crown was revealed first, afterwards Wisdom, etc., until Kingdom, which is last.

49. *Soul* (volume 2, part 2, *Inner Light*, F): The Light clothed in the Vessel of Intelligence is called "Soul." it is called thus from the term meaning "breath" since soul is the source of The Small Face which is Light of the Spirit draw-ing its existence therefrom by ascent and descent. This is the secret meaning of the verse: "And the Hayot Come and Go"; also compare the verse "And he blew the Breath of life into his nostrils"—understand this well.

50. *Encircling*: That which brings about the revelation of a level is spoken of as surrounding that level.

51. *Conclusion*: (volume 2, part 1, *Inner Light*, G^1): The fourth phase is called end or "conclusion," since it stops the Upper Light from extending to it, thereby concluding the level.

52. *Near* (volume 2, 2): Closeness of one form to another is termed "Near" to one another.

53. *Impurity* (volume 2, *Inner Reflection*, 5): A great Desire to Receive, through great Longing, is called great "Impurity," or "thickness"; less longing is called lesser "thickness." This is the phase of the Vessel wich draws the Abundance in each Countenance, termed, therefore, the interior of the Vessel.

54. *Passing* (volume 2, part 2, *Inner Light*, D^1): The illumination of a lower level must pass through the level above it. Since the lower is caused by and emerges from the upper it is considered to pass through the upper and, since it does, it is fixed there, being called "passing" Light; it does not move from there, but, instead, a kind of branch goes out of it, arriving at its place (which is to say the lower level) as one lights a candle with another candle, the first candle loosing nothing. In a similar fashion one may understand the transfer of lights from level to level. For the Light does not withdraw from place A when it comes to place B as is the case with material things, but, instead, the case is as we have explained.

55. *Upper and Lower* (volume 2, *Inner Reflection*, 86B): There are 2 fundamental distinctions we must make with re-

gard to each Countenance. They are: the Vessels which draws the Abundance in the Countenance and the Vessel which receives Abundance in the Countenance. They are absolutely, diamterically opposed to one another, for the extent of the Abundance depends on the amount of impurity in the drawing Vessel, for the larger Light in the Countenance (called Individual) requires an impurer drawing Vessel, which is to say the fourth phase of the fourth phase. The opposite is true of the receiving Vessel, for the larger Light, called Individual, is clothed only in the purest Vessel. Thus, when we distinguish Vessels which draw the Abundance, we use the terms inner and outer each inner vessel being more impure and drawing more Light, and each outer Vessel being more pure. And when we distinguish the Vessels which receive the lights in the Countenance we term them "upper and lower," the upper being the purer—a larger height being clothed in it, and the lower is impurer, a smaller height being clothed in it.

56. *Essence* (volume 2, part 2, *Inner Light*, B): The Light of Wisdom is called "Essence," because it is the Essence and "life" of an Emanation.

57. *Interiority* (volume 2, *Inner Reflection*, 86B): The impurity in the Countenance is called its "interiority," since this is the place that draws the Abundance.

58. *Interiority and Exteriority*: See Answer 55.

59. *Pipe* (volume 2, part 1, *Inner Light*, B): Vessels of Straightness are termed "Pipes," since they draw and confine the Light within themselves as a pipe confines the waters which pass through it.

60. *Line* (volume 2, part 1, *Inner Light*, B): The 10 Sefirot of the Vessels of Straightness, in terms of their Vessels, are called pipes, and in terms of the Light found in them, are called Line. Only the 10 Sefirot of the World of Primordial Man are termed a Single Line which is not the case with the World of Emanation whose 10 Sefirot have 3 lines.

61. *Erect Height* (volume 2, part 2, *Inner Light*, C): When the Lights of the Head are clothed in the Vessel of the Head we speak of the Countenance as being of "erect height."

62. *Edge* (volume 2, part 1, *Inner Light*, P): Returning Light to the extent of its own length makes an "edge" to the Upper Light, since Light does not come to the Emanation by any other Means than the enclothing of the Returning Light.

63. *Ground or Floor* (volume 2, part 2, *Inner Light*, A): The Kingdom of each level of world is termed the ground of that level or world.

64. *Head* (volume 3, 86): The 9 Sefirot of the Upper Light which extend by Binding by Striking on the Curtain of Kingdom to send up the Returning Light are called the "Head" of a level because these Lights come before the Curtain and Returning Light, and the impurity of the Curtain is unable to ascend to them (see answer 21).

65. *Spirit* (volume 2, 4): The Light clothed in the Vessel of the Small Face is called "Spirit" since its tendency is to ascend to Intelligence, drawing Abundance and to descend to Kingdom, influencing it, going from place to place as does the wind (see answer 49).

66. *Spiritual*: The word spiritual, when used to describe something in books on the Kabbalah, means that it is totally devoid of all material attributes—that is to say place, time, shape, etc. Sometimes it refers merely to the Upper Light in the Vessel even though the Vessel is also Spiritual in all its conditions.

67. *Far* (volume 2, part 1, *Inner Light*, M): An extensive change in form.

68. *Beginning of Extension* (volume 2, part 1, *Inner Light*, G): The Root of all extension of Light is called "beginning of extension," or Crown.

69. *At Once* (volume 2, part 1, *Inner Light*, F): Light which descends without devolvement from level to level of the 4 phases (since it has only one of the 4 phases) is said to descend at once; if it devolves in order of the phases its devolvement is called "slowly."

70. *The Purpose of all of These* (volume 2, part 1, *Inner Light*, G): The last phase in all of the levels, that is to say the fourth phase of the fourth phase is termed the purpose of all of these since it is the impurest of all, termed the end, and since all of the levels come only to restore it.

TABLE OF ANSWERS
TO TOPICAL QUESTIONS

71. The Endless, PB"G, is the source of the Vessels of the Circles, for these Vessels were included in the Endless, PB"G, but weren't manifest; cp. the secret meaning of the verse: "He and His name are One." (*Inner Reflection*, volume 2, 52, begin.: "It is explained above...").

72. After the Restriction, when the Light of the Endless disappeared from all 4 phases, there remained, nonetheless, a Residue in each phase on account of the Light of the Endless which was there before the Restriction (*Inner Light*, volume 2, part 1, Q, begin.: "The source...").

73. This indicates that the sole distinction is that of cause and effect alone (see answer 22) (*Inner Reflection*, volume 2, 53, begin.: "As for this...").

74. Because in the Endless, PB"G, there is no trace of a Vessel (*Inner Reflection*, op. cit.).

75. The Endless, PB"G, is the root of all the Lights in the various Worlds. (*Inner Light*, volume 2, A^1, begin.: "Which means...").

76. The Circles are the roots of all the Vessels in the various Worlds. (*Inner Light*, volume 2, part 1, Q, begin.: "From this one may...").

77. The fourth phase, called Kingdom, is the source of the Returning Light (*Inner Reflection*, volume 2, 66, begin.: "Now we shall...").

78. Because, at first, the Lights emerged in 3 phases, one beneath the other, and these 3 phases were not called Vessels, as yet—until the fourth phase was revealed, it alone being considered a Vessel. Indeed the Vessels descend from the Lights. (*Inner Reflection*, volume 2, 5, begin.: "The Spiritual Vessel...").

79. Because in the order of emanation of the Worlds from highest to lowest, we find that the *complete* always precedes and causes the revelation of the *incomplete* and in this manner the levels devolve one from the other, every lower level being inferior to the level above it, until the revelation of this World the most degraded of all (*Inner Light*, volume 2, part 1, T, begin.: "One may not...").

80. The Curtain is the first source of the Power of control in the various Worlds. (*Inner Light*, volume 2, chapter 1, 3, begin.: "The power of...").

81. It is descended from the first Restriction (*Inner Light*, volume 2, part 1, B, begin.: op. cit.).

82. Two causes preceded the Curtain: 1) the Restriction; 2) the Coming of the Light. The Curtain is revealed only when the Upper Light reaches and touches the fourth phase (see answer 43).

83. The Circles are the source of the Vessels of Straightness, since the Kingdom of the Circles drew the Light of the

Line, and by its power the Curtain was made. (*Inner Reflection*, volume 2, 56, begin.: "Now we shall explain...").

84. From the Vessels of Straightness. They themselves are unable to draw from the Endless, PB"G, since they do not have a Curtain and the necessary impurity. (*Inner Light*, volume 2, part 1, L, begin.: "And the reason...").

85. By the power of the Curtain which "impresses" them without taking along its impurity. These impressions by the Curtain are called Windows of the Circles. (*Inner Light*, volume 2, part 1, P, begin.: "This means...").

86. Since the Circles do not possess the phase of Curtain (*Inner Light*, volume 2, part 1, L, begin.: "And the reason...").

87. See above, answer 85.

88. The Light of the Line which the Circles received caused in them recognizable levels, one below the other, windows being formed in them by the impression of the Curtain; all the levels of the Line emerged in the Circles as well. (*Inner Light*, volume 2, part 2, P, begin.: "This means...").

89. Because the Vessels of Circles are at one level, with the Head of each Sefira in the Vessels of Straightness found above the Curtain, therefore they are distinguished as being found in the place of the Head of the Sefira, and they do not spread at all below the Head of Straightness, since the Vessels below Head are already found below the Curtain of Kingdom of the Head, where impurity controls them, and thus they are below the Circles (since "below" means "impure"),

since in the Circles there is neither Curtain nor impurity. Thus the Body of each Sefira is found to be void of Circles. The Ten Sefirot of the Crown of Circles all clothe the Ten Sefirot of the Head of the Crown of Straightness, and the Ten Sefirot of the Body of the Crown is void of Circles, and so the Ten Sefirot of Wisdom of Circles clothe the Ten Sefirot of the Head of the Wisdom of Straightness (and so on, in like manner.) We find then that the Body of Straightness stops between each and every Sefira of Circles; thus there is no juncture between the Sefirot of Circles, and therefore they require the Line to join them. (*Inner Light*, volume 2, part 1, C¹, begin.: "This means...").

90. The whole difference is the phase of the Curtain which Sefirot of Straightness have and Sefirot of Circles do not. (*Inner Light*, volume 2, part 1, B, begin.: "The power of control...").

91. See answer 43.

92. They are Light of the Spirit. (*Inner Light*, volume 2, part 2, L).

93. See answer 34.

94. In terms of Vessels, Circles are superior to Straightness, for the Vessels of Circles do not possess a Curtain and Impurity and Vessels of Straightness do possess a Curtain and impurity. Furthermore, the Vessels of Circles precede those of Straightness (*Inner Light*, volume 2, part 1, B, begin.: "The power of control...").

95. In terms of Lights, Straightness is superior to Circles, for the Sefirot of Straightness draw the Upper Light and influence the Circles. The Light of Straightness are called Light of the Spirit and the Lights of Circles are called Light of Life. (*Inner Light*, volume 2, part 2, L).

96. Because "exterior" means "pure," and every exterior Circle has a form closer to the form of the Endless, PB"G, it is therefore superior. (*Inner Reflection*, 7, begin.: "This is why Our Rabbi...").

97. "Interior" means "more impure," in other words, greater longing, whereby the amount of Light that is drawn is greater, and the Returning Light which is deflected is of a greater magnitude: (*Inner Reflection*, 5, begin.: "The Spiritual Vessel...").

98. Because its fourth phase does not possess impurity able to draw the Upper Light, in this respect it is the purest of all the Worlds (see answer 55). (*Inner Reflection* 13, begin.: "The World of...").

99. The Upper Light, reaching and touching the fourth phase so as to spread out in it, caused the immediate revelation of the Power of the Curtain to stop it, pushing the Light backwards (*Inner Reflection*, 18, begin.: "The answer is...").

100. When the Upper Light reached and touched the fourth phase, so as to spread out in it, then the power of Restriction was awakened, (which is the Curtain), to stop it and deflect it. (*Inner Reflection*, 56, begin.: "Now we shall explain...").

101. Because the Returning Light which the Curtain brings up is equal in quantity to the Light which wanted to spread out according to the amount of impurity in the fourth phase which means the amount of longing and drawing of the Upper Light. If the Impurity is greater, as in the fourth phase of the fourth phase, then the Light which wanted to spread out in the fourth phase is greater. If the impurity is less, as in the first phase of the fourth phase then the Light which wanted to spread out in the fourth phase is smaller. Thus the magnitude of Returning Light in the Curtain and the magnitude of impurity in the fourth phase are one and the same. (*Inner Reflection*, 60, begin.: "Therefore...").

102. Even though the Light of the Line has only 3 phases, nevertheless its Vessels of Receival derive only from the power of the fourth phase, but the fourth phase itself does not receive Light. (*Inner Reflection*, 16, begin.: "Therefore...").

103. There are two orders for the 10 Sefirot of each level: 1) from above to below beginning from Crown, ending with Kingdom—called The Ten Sefirot of Straight Light. 2) from below to above, beginning from Kingdom and ending with Crown—called Ten Sefirot of Returning Light. (*Inner Reflection*, 104, begin.: "As for the...").

104. Because this Light belongs entirely and solely to the fourth phase, which would have clothed itself in it, had not the Curtain deflected the Light, thereby becoming a phase of receival instead of the fourth phase (*Inner Reflection*, 21, begin.: "Now we can...").

105. The amount of Light which would have come to the fourth phase had not the Curtain deflected it (*Inner Reflection*, 60, begin.: "Therefore...").

106. Because the Returning Light is nothing more than the Light which would have come to the fourth phase, which is Kingdom. And since Kingdom did not receive this Light, the Light became a phase of clothing and receival for all 9 Sefirot above it, since Kingdom is the source of all Ten Sefirot of the Returning Light, being considered, therefore, the "Crown of the Returning Light" (*Inner Reflection*, 102a, begin.: "Since Kingdom...").

107. See answer 101, above.

108. See answer 101, above.

109. Because the impurity in the Curtain refers to the amount of longing in it. Therefore: "By means of the grasping and clothing of the Inner Light in the Countenance, the Surrounding Light overpowers and purifies the Impurity in the Curtain." (*Inner Reflection*, 74, begin.: "The reason...").

110. Since the Circles do not have a Curtain and Impurity, they have no Vessel to draw the Upper Light, receiving their Light by means of the Vessels of Straightness; their Lights are therefore called "Light of Life," that is to say: this Light does not have the power to influence, but is sufficient unto itself alone. (*Inner Reflection*, 95, begin.: "Thus the Light...").

111. Because the Vessels of Straightness have a Curtain and Impurity they are able to draw the Upper Light, and

influence other Sefirot. Light which influences is called "Light of Spirit," or Male Light. (*Inner Light*, volume 2, part 2, L).

112. The first three Sefirot are void of the impurity of the Curtain since the Curtain and Kingdom are the last phase that they contain; impurity can never ascend to them since it can't go higher than its place. One must know that the first 3 Sefirot, KH''B, refers to the Head of the Level (see answer 13) which contains ten complete Sefirot. (*Inner Light*, volume 2, part 1, R, begin.: "The reason for this...").

113. Each and every Sefira is defined as having a Head termed the First three Sefirot and a Body termed the Bottom Seven Sefirot (see answer 64). The Sefira of Crown has the First 3 Sefirot and the Seven Lower Sefirot. The same is true of Wisdom which has the first 3 Sefirot and Lower Seven Sefirot; the same is true of Intelligence, etc. The place where we find all ten sefirot of the first (top) 3 and Bottom Seven Sefirot of Circles is in the Head and First 3 of Straightness alone, because the Ten Sefirot of Circles of the Sefira of Crown surround only the first 3 of the Crown of Straightness, the Bottom Seven Sefirot of Crown of Straightness being void of Circles (see answer 89). Thus all 10 Sefirot of Wisdom of Circles surround only the first 3 Sefirot of Wisdom of Straightness, the 7 Bottom Sefirot of Wisdom of Straightness being void of Circles; thus with all the Sefirot. (*Inner Light*, volume 2, part 1, R, begin.: "It has been...").

114. Since neither have anything of the Impurity of the Curtain, whatsoever (see answer 89). (*Inner Light*, volume 2, chapter 1, R, begin.: "The reason...").

115. The distance of the 7 Bottom Sefirot of the Sefirot of Straightness serves as the border between each and every Circle. Thus the 7 Bottom Sefirot of the Crown of Straightness separate the 10 Sefirot of the Circle of Crown from the Circle of Wisdom; the 7 Bottom Sefirot of the Sefirot of Wisdom of Straightness separate the 10 Sefirot of the Circle of Wisdom from the Circle of Intelligence, and so on, in this manner (see answer 89). (*Inner Light,* volume 2, part 1, R, begin.: "It has been...").

116. See answer 89.

117. Because Lights preceded the Vessels (see answer 13) and the Returning Light which ascends from below to above and clothes the Vessels is not considered an actual phase of Vessels, but the root of Vessels, and we are unable to grasp Light without a Vessel (see answer 21).

118. Even the top 3 Sefirot of the Level are further distinguished as possessing top 3 and Bottom 7 Sefirot; we are permitted to deal with the 7 Bottom Sefirot of the first three Sefirot (*Inner Light,* volume 2, part 2, E[1], begin.: "The Interior refers...").

119. Since they are in the phase of the top 3 Sefirot, and so all 10 Sefirot of Circles are established in the three top Sefirot of Straightness (see answer 13 above).

120. The root of the 4 phases is called Crown, the first phase is called Wisdom, the second phase is Intelligence, the third phase is called Beauty, or the Small Face, which includes in itself 6 Sefirot: Mercy, Judgement, Beauty, Lasting En-

durance, Majesty, Foundation. The fourth phase is called Kingdom.

121. This teaches us that even though the fourth phase, Kingdom, receives nothing from the Upper Light after the Restriction, nevertheless, because of the Attribute of the Returning Light in the fourth phase, it is considered to be as important as the other Sefirot—thus "ten, not nine." "Ten, not eleven," this teaches us, furthermore, that we should not imagine that the fourth phase also has some phase of Receival of Upper Light. If so, Kingdom would be 2 Sefirot: Kingdom of Straight Light and Kingdom of Returning Light, making the total 11. Therefore we are cautioned: "Ten, not eleven," for Kingdom receives no Light whatsoever from the Straight Light.

122. Since it is opposite from its Root, whose form is to influence, whereas the fourth phase's form is to receive, and since 2 opposites cannot stand in a cause and effect relationship there must be gradual devolvement from level to level, for the Root is the immediate cause of phase 1 which is closest to it, phase 1 causes phase 2, phase 2 causes phase 3. After the third phase, the fourth is now able to follow. (*Inner Reflection*, chapter 1, 5, begin.: "The Spiritual Vessel...").

123. Because impurity is the major drawing and receiving Vessel, by means of the Returning Light which it sends up, therefore the impurity in the Vessel is considered its interior. The less impure is considered exterior, and the purest is considered the absolute exterior (see answer 55). (*Inner Reflection*, chapter 1, 5, begin.: "The Spiritual Vessel...").

124. Compare the layers of wood in a vessel made of 4 concentric layers: that which fills the Vessel touches only the innermost layer in the Vessel. (*Inner Reflection*, chapter 1, 5, begin.: "The Spiritual Vessel...").

125. The size of the Returning Light sent up by the Curtain of the level or world in question. (*Inner Reflection*, chapter 6, 65, begin.: "From what has...").

126. Because the Vessel of Receival for all 4 phases is the fourth phase alone, the 3 other phases do not have the power to draw or receive, whatsoever. Therefore, because the fourth phase restricted itself not to receive, the first 3 phases also remained without a Vessel of Receival, thus their Lights also disappeared. (*Inner Reflection*, chapter 2, 16, begin.: "Therefore...").

127. A) The essence of the Material of the Vessel, which is to say the amount of its impurity.

B) The power of Restriction which resides in the fourth phase in its impurity.

C) The Curtain (see answer 43).

There are 2 further divisions of A: 1) The first material in the Vessel, which is to say the phase of Kingdom of the preceding level, considered cause and Emanator distinguished before the Light reaches the level emanated; 2) the material itself of the emanated level itself, after the Light destined for the Emanated level reaches it (*Inner Reflection*, chapter 3, 24, begin.: "These Vessels..."; 27, begin.: "Now we will...").

128. A) That which is thought of as Kingdom of the Upper.

B) That which is though of as the material of the emanated level itself (see answer 127, above).

129. As long as the emanated level has not received the Light destined for it, it is considered in terms of Kingdom of the level above it (see answer 127).

130. When the emanated level grasps its Light, from that time it is considered to have emerged from the domain of the Kingdom of the Upper level, termed Emanator, and to have arrived at its own domain (see answer 127).

131. Necessary receival is termed "Not possible;" this refers especially to the Light of Wisdom or the Illumination of Wisdom, considered an essential, vital phase of the Countenance, whereby: "It is impossible for the Countenance to separate from it." Compare a man forced to guard his life and continued existence. (*Inner Reflection*, chapter 4, 46, begin.: "Phase three...").

132. Longing is termed "Intending," since of a thing which one longs to receive, we say one has fixed his heart firmly to draw it—since longing is felt in the heart, and the intention is in the heart. But this holds true only when the Light is lacking, not when there is Light, which we call "Not intending." (*Inner Reflection*, chapter 4, 43, begin.: "Now we may...").

133. Because only the Light of Wisdom is destined for phase 1, which is the life and essence of the Countenance,

therefore it is considered "not Possible," because it must receive its life and essence—and necessary receival is not receival. Thus no Longing is revealed in it after the Light of Wisdom since longing is not revealed when the phase is full of Light but when there is no Light and it longs to grasp it (Light). (*Inner Reflection*, chapter 4, 43, begin.: "Now we may...").

134. Because phase 2 is the awakening of the Desire to influence which thereby draws the Light of Mercy; but it is not forced to awaken thus, and it would have been "Possible" to separate from it completely—thus we term it "Possible." However there is also the phase of "Not Intending," since the aforementioned longing must be for the Light of Wisdom alone, not for the Light of Mercy, since the desire for the Light of Mercy is not considered impurity, because the Restriction effected only the Light of Wisdom, not at all the Light of Mercy. Thus the Longing for the Light of Mercy is not called "Intention."

135. The third phase involves the drawing of the Illumination of Wisdom into the Light of Mercy which was drawn by Intelligence—this drawing is called "Not Possible," because the Illumination of Wisdom is a receival necessary for the Countenance. It is called "Intending" because this drawing took place when the Illumination of Wisdom was lacking, which caused Longing (in phase 3).

136. After the Illumination of Wisdom in the 3rd phase, there was no need for a new awakening after the substance of the Light of Wisdom, because the Illumination of Wisdom

is alone entirely sufficient for the existence of the third phase; thus this drawing is considered "Possible," since the third phase could be separated from it; it is considered "Intending," since phase 3 lacks the substance of the Light of Wisdom which it drew, experiencing great longing when drawing it.

137. Since a complete Vessel must have a phase of Longing to Receive, which is revealed only under 2 conditions: Possible, and Intending (see above, answer 136).

138. The rule is that the Upper Light does not cease to illumine the Emanations for even a moment, but whenever a drawing Vessel is fittingly revealed, the Upper Light illumines it at once. Thus after the phase of drawing of the fourth phase of the fourth phase has been filled, thereby giving birth to a new vessel of drawing, which has the phase of impurity of the third phase of the fourth phase, then it too is at once filled by the Upper Light. Afterwards when a new phase of the impurity of phase 2 of phase 4 has been emanated and has emerged, it too is filled at once with the Upper Light. And so on, always.

139. Because the Upper Light is always at absolute rest, without any renewal of form, since renewal in Spiritual Substance is considered movement, and all renewals of form effected in the spreading of the Upper Light are by the power of drawing revealed in the Emanation alone (see volume 1, answer 64)—and even this spreading of the Upper Light is only in a manner resembling the lighting of one candle by another: the first loses nothing.—Thus, only that part of the spreading Upper Light which was received by the Emanation

receives a new form, in a reciprocal relationship between the Vessel and the Light clothed in it—but the Upper Light loses nothing, and is in no way renewed by this spreading which reached the Emanation.

140. The difference is one of antithesis. For the phase of influencing of the Upper Light the Countenance must have a great deal of impurity, the largest amount in existence, because only then can it extend the largest and fullest Light. But the clothing of the Upper Light in the Vessels is exactly opposite, because the largest and fullest Light is clothed only in the purest vessel in existence. Thus we must always distinguish the two aspects discussed above, with respect to every Countenance: the phase of Influence resident in the extra impurity is discussed in terms of Inferior and Exterior, and, Receival and Clothing in the Vessels is discussed in terms of higher or lower. Thus the largest Countenance in existence must be the most Interior, which means the impurest of all Countenances in existence. Moreover it must be the highest Countenance in existence, which means the purest of all Countenances in existence. For they are 2 distinct Vessels: one to draw the Light, one to receive it (see above, answer 55, and below, answer 141).

141. Because the Upper Light is not seized in the Countenance unless according to the amount of the Returning Light which ascends from the Curtain in the Countenance, and its extent depends on the impurity in the fourth phase (see above answer 101, and answer 2). Thus the influencing agent must have more impurity than the lower. This is not true of the Receiving (Sefira) which requires the purest Vessel so that the

Light can be clothed in it, i.e., so that there can be equality of form between the Light and the Vessel, because the change in form between them distances the Light from the Vessels (see above, answer 16, and answer 140).

142. See above, answer 139.

143. The Upper Light has, perforce, a Desire to Influence, a Desire which is distinguished as a final phase in the Upper Light, this being the section (i.e. the aforesaid Desire to Influence) which is changed into a phase of drawing Light, of phase 1, since this phase of drawing Light is certainly a renewal of form in the Desire to Influence and is thus distinguished as dividing in itself and emerging from the phase of the Desire to Influence, becoming the first phase of the Desire to Receive, in other words: it emerges from the phase of Emanator to the phase of Emanation, since a change in form separates and distances Spiritual Substances from one another, as is well known. However the distinction of "Part" does not lessen at all the "whole," but instead, as when one candle is used to light another, the first is not at all diminished; understand this well.

144. When we are distinguishing the materials in the Vessels we define them in terms of 4 phases, and when we wish to include the Residues in each and every Vessel we define them by the names KH"BZ"N.

145. First, the smaller enter, then the larger, first Life, then Spirit, etc. finally Individual (see answer 48).

146. First, the most important Vessels grow, then the small Vessels, first Crown, then Wisdom, etc., finally the Vessel of Kingdom which comes last.

147. Kingdom of the Upper, which becomes Crown for the Lower, that is to say, the Desire to Influence in the Upper, becomes the first substance in the Lower (see answer 143).

148. The root of the 4 phases is called the Crown of the 10 Sefirot of the Straight Light in a level; Kingdom of a level is the Crown of the 10 Sefirot of the Returning Light at that Level.

149. Because if there were change or substitution it would not be eternal; the matter is simple.

150. This is by means of the 10 Sefirot of Straight Light, since all Light is drawn only from the Endless, PB''G, and so the lower must pass through all those above it, in the manner of cause and effect, until it reaches the lowest effect to which the Light reaches. As a result of the fact that the Light does not disappear from place A when it moves to place B each Sefira is fixed with all the Lights which pass through it.

151. This is by means of the 10 Sefirot of the Returning Light, whose Root and Crown is considered to be Kingdom (see above, answer 148), when all sections of the Returning Light which clothe those Sefirot above it pass from below to above—thus every lower Sefira comprises all sections of the Returning Light which belong to the Sefirot above it.

152. The inclusion of Sefirot one inside the other, so that each Sefira is made of Ten Sefirot, these ten also being made

of ten Sefirot, and so on, *ad infinitum*, is by means of the 2 paths of the 10 Sefirot of Straight Light and the 10 Sefirot of Returning Light which exist at every level (see answer 20). We must find the key to figure out easily the shifts in order of the ten secondary Sefirot in a Sefira on account of this phenomenon of inclusion, rather than on account of the very nature of the Sefira itself. Therefore, remember the following 3 principles always to be applied. For example, if we wish to determine the 10 Sefirot included in Intelligence: The first principle is that there are 2 essential Sefirot in Intelligence, Intelligence of the Straight Light and Majesty of the Returning Light. Second, count the Sefirot downwards to the Foundation, these being the Straight Light it contains, in this case: HG''T NH''Y which pass through it from above to below. Third: count the Sefirot upward to the Crown, in this case 2: Foundation and Kingdom, and you have ascertained the Sefirot of its Returning Light which pass through it from below to above. Now we have considered its 2 essential Sefirot, 6 of the Straight Light, and 2 of the Returning Light—10 in all. In this manner one may calculate for each Sefira and know at a glance all the phases included in it.

153. Nine of Straight Light from Crown to Foundation, and one of Returning Light, which is Kingdom alone.

154. Eight of Straight Light from Wisdom to Foundation, which are clothed in the purest Vessels, so that the Light of Wisdom is clothed in the Vessel of Crown, etc., and two of Returning Light, Foundation and Kingdom clothed in the Vessels of Foundation and Kingdom.

155. Seven of Straight Light, from Intelligence downwards here too the Light of Intelligence in the Vessel of Crown, etc. until the Light of Foundation in the Vessel of Lasting Endurance. Three of Returning Light, Majesty, Foundation, and Kingdom in the Vessels of Majesty, Foundation, and Kingdom.

156. Six of Straight Light from Mercy to Foundation, and 4 of Returning Light from Lasting Endurance to Kingdom, the Returning Light of Lasting Endurance in the Vessel of Lasting Endurance etc.

157. Five of Straight Light from Judgement to Foundation and 5 of Returning Light from Beauty to Kingdom, clothed in the manner described above, Straight Light in the purest Vessels and Returning Light each in the Vessel appropriate to it.

158. Four of Straight Light from Beauty to Foundation, and 6 of Returning Light from Judgement to Kingdom.

159. Three of Straight Light from Lasting Endurance to Foundation, and seven of Returning Light from Mercy to Kingdom.

160. Two of Straight Light from Majesty to Foundation, and 8 of Returning Light from Intelligence to Kingdom.

161. One of Straight Light, Foundation, and 9 of Returning Light from Wisdom to Kingdom.

162. Ten of Returning Light alone, without any Straight Light.

163. Nine of Straight Light from Crown to Foundation and 1 of Returning Light, Kingdom.

164. Eight of Straight Light from Wisdom to Kingdom, and 2 of Returning Light, Foundation and Kingdom.

165. Seven of Straight Light from Intelligence to Kingdom, and 3 of Returning Light, from Majesty to Kingdom.

166. Six of Straight Light from Mercy to Foundation, and 4 of Returning Light from Lasting Endurance to Kingdom.

167. First we must understand the 10 secondary Sefirot included in the primary Lasting Endurance, which are: 3 of Straight Light: the Light of Lasting Endurance is clothed in the Vessel of the Crown of the primary Lasting Endurance, the Light of Majesty in the Vessel of Wisdom of the primary Lasting Endurance, and the Light of Foundation in the Vessel of Intelligence; now take the secondary Wisdom of the primary Lasting Endurance, it too necessarily including 10 Sefirot—8 of Straight Light which pass through it from above to below—even in those which have only Returning Light, because when the Sefirot are inclusive, the Sefirot of Straight Light always shine into the Sefirot which contain Returning Light, however the 8 Sefirot of Straight Light that passed from Wisdom downwards are not a phase of Light of Wisdom but Light of Majesty, since Light of Majesty is clothed in the Vessel of Wisdom in the primary Lasting Endurance as explained above; thus there are now in the 10 Sefirot of Wisdom of Lasting Endurance only Straight Lights which pass from Wisdom of Majesty downwards, since Wisdom of Majesty is in the Vessel of Crown, and Intelligence of Majesty in Wis-

dom, and Mercy of Majesty in Intelligence, and Judgement of Majesty in Mercy, Beauty of Majesty in Judgement. Thus we know that in Judgement of Wisdom of Lasting Endurance there is Straight Light from the Light of Beauty of Majesty. Now we take this Judgement of Wisdom of Lasting Endurance which also necessarily included 10 secondary Sefirot: from Straight Light which passes through it from above to below, and from Returning Light which passes through it from below to above. Thus it contains 5 Sefirot of Straight Light from Judgement downwards, but this is by no means Light of Judgement, but rather 5 lower phases of the Light of Beauty of Majesty, clothed in the purest Vessels, and so the Light of Judgement of Beauty of Majesty is clothed in the Vessel of Crown of Judgement of Wisdom of Lasting Endurance. And the Light of Beauty of Beauty of Majesty is clothed in the Vessel of Wisdom of the Judgement of Wisdom of Lasting Endurance; and the Light of Lasting Endurance of Beauty of Majesty is clothed in the Vessel of Intelligence of Judgement of Wisdom of Lasting Endurance; and the Light of Majesty of Beauty of Majesty is clothed in the Vessel of Mercy of Judgement of Wisdom of Lasting Endurance. The Light of Foundation of Beauty of Majesty is clothed in the Vessel of Judgement of Judgement of Wisdom of Lasting Endurance. There are, furthermore, 5 Sefirot of Returning Light which are clothed in their appropriate vessels, as always.

168. If we examine Intelligence of Majesty, we find that it contains only Returning Light without Straight Light, however the Straight Light of the nearby Light of Foundation illumines it; and so this Intelligence is also comprised of Lights

which pass through it, 7 of Straight Light from Intelligence downwards. Because the Light in it is only the Light of Foundation of Straight Light (as explained above), thus its Straight Light begins from Intelligence of Foundation downwards, with the Light of Intelligence of Foundation clothed in the Vessel of Crown, and so on, and the Light of Majesty of Foundation in the Vessel of Beauty of Intelligence of the primary Majesty. Afterwards, when we take the secondary Beauty of Intelligence of Majesty mentioned above, it too comprised of 10 Sefirot, one finds 4 of Straight Light from Beauty downwards, clothed in the uppermost Vessels, as follows: Beauty of Foundation of Foundation in the Vessel of Crown; Lasting Endurance of Foundation of Foundation in the Vessel of Wisdom; Majesty of Foundation of Foundation in the Vessel of Intelligence; and Foundation of Foundation of Foundation in the Vessel of Mercy—there are, furthermore, 6 phases of Returning Light which pass through it from below to above, from Judgement to Kingdom, clothed in their respective Vessels, as usual.

169. If we first take Foundation of Crown, we find that its 10 Sefirot contain only the Light of Foundation in the Vessel of Crown, the remaining Lights being Returning Light. When we take Lasting Endurance of Foundation of Crown, we find only Returning Light, but the Light of Foundation of Straight Light in the Crown shines there, and Lasting Endurance of Foundation of the Crown is distinguished in the phase of Straight Light of Foundation, and when it is comprised of 10 Sefirot, it contains 3 Lights (of Straightness): Lasting Endurance, Majesty, Foundation, downwards to the

Foundation, which pass from above to below from the phase of Foundation of Straight Light, clothed as follows: Lasting Endurance of Foundation in the Vessel of Crown, Majesty of Foundation in the Vessel of Wisdom, Foundation of Foundation in the Vessel of Intelligence, and 7 of Returning Light HG"T NHY"M, according to their respective Vessels, as explained above.

170. It has only Returning Light, since everything extended from Kingdom has only Returning Light.

171. The rule is: the most important Lights are clothed in the purest Vessels, the least important Lights are clothed in the impurest Vessels. Thus, in the Sefira of Crown, the Kingdom of Returning Light is clothed in Kingdom of Crown. In the Sefira of Wisdom, the 8 Sefirot of Straight Light, H"B, HG"T, NH"Y, are clothed in the Vessels KH"B, HG"T, N"H, while Foundation and Kingdom of Returning Light are clothed in Foundation and Kingdom (in the Sefira of Wisdom). In the Sefira of Intelligence the 7 Sefirot of Straight Light in Intelligence HG"T, NH"Y are clothed in the Vessels KH"B HG"T and Lasting Endurance, and Majesty, Foundation, Kingdom of Returning Light are clothed in Majesty, Foundation, and Kingdom (in the Sefira of Intelligence) and so on, in like manner.

172. There are 10 causes. They are as follows:

1) The cause of all the causes is The Endless, PB"G, which cause the 4 phases to be recognizable after the Restriction of the Light. But in the Endless, PB"G, alone no Vessel is distinguished, since it is entirely made of Light. However only

from the lower, from the world of Restriction, can we learn about the Upper.

2) The first three phases, caused one by the other, are distinguished as the cause of the Revelation of the potential for Desiring equality of form in the fourth phase, termed Kingdom of the Endless, PB''G.

3) Kingdom of the Endless is the cause of Crown in the World of Restriction, because that phase of Desire to Desire equality of form which Kingdom of the Endless received became a change of form in Kingdom of the Endless, PB''G, and divides from Kingdom of the Endless, emerging on its own outside of Kingdom, becoming Crown of the World of Restriction. (See Answer 32, above—read it carefully).

4) This Crown causes the first Restriction, since it spreads anew to its fourth phase (see answer 38), then it restricted the Desire to Receive, and the Light departed.

5) The departure of the Light after the Restriction causes the Revelation of the Vessels of the Ten Sefirot of Circles (see answer 72).

6) The Vessel of Kingdom of Circles, their fourth phase, causes the renewed drawing of the Upper Light from the Endless PB''G (see answer 83, and 138).

7) The Upper Light drawn anew causes the Revelation of the Power of the Curtain in the Vessel of Kingdom (see answer 43).

8) The Curtain causes the 10 Sefirot of Returning Light which ascend from it upwards to the Crown of Straight Light; they are called Head of Primordial Man (see answer 101).

9) The Returning Light which ascends from the Curtain causes the Revelation of the Vessels of Straightness, which is to say it gives the Power of spreading in the fourth phase to spread to its own 10 Sefirot and reach to Kingdom of Kingdom.

10) The above mentioned fourth phase which received the Power of spreading from the Returning Light causes the 10 Sefirot of the Vessels of Primordial Man called the Body of Primordial Man, up until its phase of Kingdom (see answer 11).

The End (With God's Help) of Volume 2

"LOVE YOUR FELLOWMAN AS YOURSELF"

According to the Kabbalah the universe resides in a system where an effect is a result of a cause which is indirect, but is neither random nor accidental. The root of this causality is imbedded in the creation and constitutes a passage to the physical realm. Within the chain of "cause and effect" is found the life of man, and everything which happens in it. If man will see and understand this chain, he will know how to direct his life towards his goal through the easiest and best path, and will know to implement in a balanced way the love of his fellowman, as it is written, "Love your fellowman as yourself".

"...and after forty days that the column will rise from the earth to the heavens in front of the eyes of the whole world the Mashiach will be revealed. From the East side a star will shine in surround this star and will make war with it from all the sides, three times a day for seventy days. And all the people of the world will see..." (Zohar, 'Shemot' part 101).

THE WISDOM OF KABBALAH AND THE AGE OF AQUARIUS

The wisdom of Kabbalah dates from thousands of years ago and has accompanied the world since its creation. The sages of Kabbalah have used its hidden knowledge in order to analyze and understand the reason for the universe and the reason for life. Today, in the age of Aquarius, the age of revelations and discoveries, this wisdom is being revealed to the public at large. The wisdom of Kabbalah, which is of "the ancient days", comes to develop whatever is found beyond the five senses of man, and reveals the tremendous forces which are hidden within him. It enlightens the miraculous harmony which exists in the universe and in our world, and directs each person to the harmonious path which is within his own life, and to the harmony which exists between himself and his fellowman.

THE ANSWER TO THE ESSENCE OF LIFE

Kabbalah is the hidden knowledge of Judaism. Kabbalah sees in Judaism an expression of absolute perfection of the universe, not by way of simply relating to the writings of Judaism in their external sense, but by penetrating to the very depth of truth. With the guidance of the book of Zohar written by Rabbi Shimon bar Yochai, it becomes possible for us to reach the essence of things, understand their roots, and directly reveal the solution to problems. Usually man relates to life within the framework of effects and results which are a collection of secondary branches, and which impede man's more basic, primary vision of the complete chain of events. The Kabbalah teaches us to see how the bridges are built between that which is in the Zohar concerning the past, present, and future, and the bridges upon which we have arrived today. The book of Zohar, with an intense light, illuminates the path which leads to the true solution of any problem from the most simple to the most complex.

"There is no question in the universe to which you will not find an answer in the teachings of Kabbalah" Rabbi Dr. P.S. Berg.

COURSES OFFERED IN THE RESEARCH CENTRE OF KABBALAH

It is the privilege of every man to reach the most elevated heights of understanding himself and the universe around him. The way to this understanding is through the teachings of Kabbalah. The Research Centre of Kabbalah presents courses in various fields of Kabbalah and studies in different levels of Zohar ranging from beginners to advanced levels. The following is a list of courses offered in the Research Centre of Kabbalah with a brief description of each course.

*   Kabbalah Basic Course

This course includes the definition of terms and an introduction of understanding the principles of Kabbalah. It also includes concepts which are in effect the primary keys to the teaching of mysticism. This course represents an indispensable basis for the rest of the subjects which are taught in the Centre, even to the most advanced levels of Kabbalah studies.

*   Kabbalistic Meditation

Kabbalistic meditation is a method of self-reflection dating from ancient days. It is based on the method of the previous Kabbalists and has been unified and simplified by the saintly ARI, Rabbi Yitzhak Luria, one of the great Kabbalists of Safed. This is a practical method which brings us to high levels of awareness and to the true evaluation of the forces which are hidden in man. Kabbalistic meditation acquires for us the tools necessary for bridging the gap between the foces of the soul and the forces of the body, and brings us to a growing utilization of the potential that is imbedded in us.

*   Reincarnation and Life After Death

The Kabbalah sees in life not only a process of birth and death, but a continuous chain of cycles in which the soul (the inner energy of man) enters this world to fulfill a particular duty, and "leaves" it several times. The soul returns to the process of life many times in different bodies, up to the point where she reaches a perfect completion of the duty which has been assigned to her.

The understanding of this process leads to the understanding of all the processes which take place in the life of man. During his life time a man may ask himself who he is, why he was born to particular parents in a particular neighborhood; he is called by a name that was "fixed" for him, and finds himself in a particular society to fulfill a particular duty. Why does he meet a particular spouse to bring into the world children with particular personalities and the like? There awaits to be revealed an amazing composition of a picture of a puzzle which when seen explains to us every instant of our lives, and also explains the historical process of life and the world, from its creation to its completion.

"...and in the sixth century of the sixth millenium the gates of wisdom above and the spring of wisdom below will open..." (Zohar, 'Vayera' Part 445).

ADDITIONAL COURSES

*   Kabbalah for the Advanced
    This course embraces deeper concepts in the wisdom of the hidden in order to understand the complementing image of the universe in which man is the center.

*   Reincarnation for the Advanced
    the technique for discovery of previous incarnation.

*   Kabbalistic Astrology

*   Meditation for the Advanced
    The relation between Kabbalistic meditation and Kabbalistic astrology.

*   Essence of Hebrew Letters Their Forces

*   The Week in Zohar
    A course that explains the cosmic influence of every week of the year according to the Zohar.

*   Study of the book "Study of the Ten Emanations"

*   Study of the books "Tree of Life" and "Zohar"

*   Kabbalah and Naturalism

*   History of the Kabbalah in Aggadah and in Mysticism

*   The Mystic Aggadah

IS'NT THE KABBALAH STUDY ONLY FOR THOSE OVER 40?

It is commonly heard that the study of Kabbalah is permitted only to people over 40 years of age, and only to individuals who have "filled themselves with the six books of Mishnah and Poskim" and to any other the study of Kabbalah is likely to cause mental and/or emotional imbalance.

This argument is erroneous and in essence has no basis at all. The precise explanation of this argument is as follows: The Kabbalah has two components, "Sitrei Torah" and "Taamei Torah". The study of the "Taamei Torah" deals with the development of inner forces which are imbedded in man and bring him to understanding and seeing the essence of life and the essence of the universe. The study content of the "Taamei Torah" is understandable to every one that desires to study it. While "Sitrei Torah" deals with the secretive studies of the Kabbalah and is reserved only for those who have worked up to the point at which they can sufficiently cope with the forces which are in those secrets.

It is important to understand that the prerequisites of age and spiritual development which are mentioned above relate only to the study of "Sitrei Torah" and there is no prohibition, danger, or doubt whatsoever in regard to the study of "Taamei Torah" in Kabbalah at any age.

The person who has acquired a large and deep knowledge in Kabbalah and is ready to study the secrets of the Torah, in that case will be found by the teacher who will teach him!!!

The Research Centre of Kabbalah is an autonomous and non-profit organization which was established in 1922. Its goal is to publicize the wisdom of Kabbalah and the essence of Judaism to the public at large by way of public lectures, classes, and seminars. The Centre prints and publishes in Hebrew, English, and other languages, ancient and modern Kabbalistic literature, written by the early and later Kabbalists.

Public activities such as spiritual site-seeings, Shabbat and Holy Days gatherings, and seminars on various subjects are organized.

The Centre has several branches in Israel. The main branch is in Tel-Aviv, and publicizes the wisdom of Kabbalah in Jerusalem, Haifa, Safed, Kfar Saba, and also abroad in New York and Los Angeles.

The Centre with all its branches in Israel is open to the public to learn, hear, ask, and become interested in the wisdom of Kabbalah. You are invited to visit any of the branches.

For more information write or call:

THE RESEARCH CENTRE OF KABBALAH

25 Bugrashov Street
Tel-Aviv, ISRAEL 63342
Tel: (03)280-570

200 Park Ave. Suite 303E
New York, N.Y. 10017
Tel: (212)986-2515

Books in English

1. ■ **Kabbalah for the Layman** by Dr. Philip S. Berg.
   *The basic concepts of Kabbalah
   presented in a simple manner.*

2. ■ **The Kabbalah Connection** by Dr. Philip S. Berg.
   A Spiritual Guide to the Cosmic Connection.

3. ■ **An Echo of the Future** by Dr. Philip S. Berg.
   A Guide to Kabbalistic Astrology.

4. ■ **The Wheels of a Soul** by Dr. Philip S. Berg.
   A Gateway to Kabbalistic Reincarnation.

5. ■ **An Entrance to the Zohar** by Rabbi Yehuda Ashlag.
   *A Collection of forward-looking introductions
   to the study of Kabbalah.
   Edited and compiled by Dr. Philip S. Berg.*

6. ■ **An Entrance to the Tree of LIfe**
   by Rabbi Yehuda Ashlag
   Edited and compiled by Dr. Philip S. Berg.

7. ■ **Ten Luminous Emanations (Talmud Eser Sefirot)**
   By Rabbi Yehuda Ashlag
   *Vol. 1 Interpretation of the Sefirot or Heavenly
   Attributes according to the system of Rabbi Yitzhak
   Luria. known as the Ari — Edition also contains
   Hebrew-to-English text of the Ari's
   ETZ CHAIM (TREE OF LIFE).*

8. ■ **Ten Luminous Emanations (Talmud Eser Sefirot)**
   by Rabbi Yehuda Ashlag
   Vol. II Edited and compiled by Dr. Philip S. Berg.

9. ■ **General Principles of Kabbalah**
   by Rabbi Moses Luzzatto
   An early 18th Century text in the Lurianic Tradition.

10. ■ **The Light of Redemption**
    by Rabbi Levi Krakovski
    An introduction to the basic concepts of Kabbalah.

11. ■ **Sefer Ha-Zohar — The Book of Splendour**
by Rabbi Shimon Bar Yochai.
English translation — five volumes.

12. ■ **Heaven on Your Head:** by Rabbi S. Z. Kahana
*Esoteric Stories related to mystical experiences
in the Holy Land.*

13. ■ **The Talmud in English:**
*This is a classic in Early Hebrew Education:
Set in 18 Volumes, certainly a library piece.*

14. ■ **Legends of Zion:**
*Tales on this focal point of spiritual energy.
Enlarge your prospectus of great history which occurred
at this place.* Dr. S. Z. Kahana

15. ■ **Legends of Israel:**
*A more broader spectrum of spiritual and esoteric
legend surrounding the Holy Land.* Dr. S. Kahana

16. ■ **Anthology of Jewish Mysicism:**
*Translated from the Hebrew by Raphael Ben Zion.
A different approach to this wonderous teaching.
A fine work even for the uninitiated.*

The Sefirot

and

The Twelve Tribes, Months and Astrological Signs

We have learnt that Biblical narrative is the outer covering for many inner levels of concealed truths. An example of this is the story of Jacob and his twelve sons, who became the leaders of the twelve tribes of Israel. The chariot of the bottled-up energy (sefira) of Tiferet contains six sefirot-Hesed, Gevurah, Tiferet, Netzah, Hod, Yesod. Each of these sefirot in its male and female aspect can be attributed to one of the twelve sons, to the twelve months of the year, and to their astrological signs. Of the remaining four sefirot (Keter, Hokhmah, Binah, Malkhut), the upper three have no direct influence on this mundane level of existence, while Malkhut represents the Desire to Receive — Man himself, who is the ultimate recipient of all these energies.

The list below, which is derived from the words of Torah concerning the blessing given by Jacob to his sons, is presented for the reader's interest and information. A more detailed discussion of the subject will be found in a future volume on Astrology and the Kabbalah.

Sefira	Tribe	Months
Hesed	Reuben	Nissan
Gevurah	Shimon	Iyar
Tiferet	Levi	Sivan
Netzah	Yehuda	Tamuz
Hod	Yisechar	Av
Yesod	Zebulun	Elul
Hesed	Binyamin	Tishrei
Gevurah	Dan	Marhesvon
Tiferet	Naftali	Kislev
Netzah	Gad	Tevet
Hod	Asher	Shevat
Yesod	Yosef	Adar

Sign	English	Solar Equivalent
Taleh	Lamb	Aries
Shor	Ox	Taurus
Ti'umin	Twins	Gemini
Sartan	Crab	Cancer
Aryeh	Lion	Leo
Betulah	Virgin	Virgo
Ma'oznaim	Scales	Libra
Akrav	Scorpion	Scorpio
Keshet	Rainbow	Sagittarius
G'di	Goat	Capricorn
D'li	Vessel	Aquarius
Dagim	Fish	Pisces

The Magen David

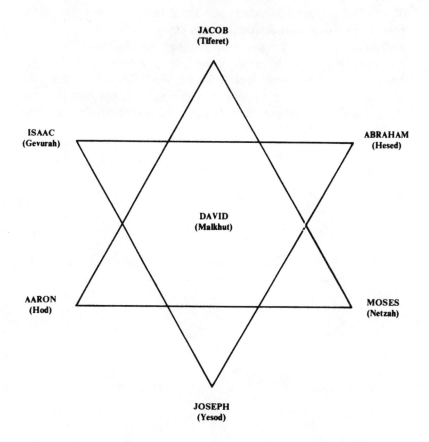

The Shield of David, in a broader sense, implies the concept of cosmic consciousness. When a thorough knowledge of the Upper and Lower Triads has been achieved, then one can reach a Devekut with the cosmos which is represented by the Shield of David. Cosmic influences, namely the seven basic planets together with the twelve signs of the Zodiac are directly related and bound up with the above seven Sefirot. Each Sefirah is considered the internal energy of the seven planets which are as follows: Saturn, Jupiter, Mars, Sun, Venus, Mercury and the Moon in this order. Each planet rules over and dominates two signs of the Zodiac. The sun and moon rule over but one sign. Through Kabbalistic Meditation, one can connect with cosmic consciousness thereby achieving a level of pure awareness. When the individual has mastered the art of direct communion with and an attachment to the interiority of these cosmic influences, the Sefirot, then it is the individual who can now *direct* his destiny.